Love. Louder.

A Memoir of the 60s

By Peter Berliner

With Larry Horwitz and Jay M. Levy

"Bob Ochsman will be wealthy. You and I won't. Levy will never be very happy. I will. I love too much. You don't love loudly enough." — Larry Horwitz

"Everyone here exists on memories." — Jay M. Levy

Contact the author: _plberliner@gmail.com_

Cover design: Barbara Erwine

ISBN # 978-1-387-24134-7

Foreword

The genesis of this book was the unearthing of a collection of letters I exchanged with two friends while I was in college. They had been kept, along with some travel journals, in a cardboard box that had been moved from Indiana to Ohio and Colorado, then to Seattle, over a span of nearly five decades.

When put in chronological order, the letters—some typed and others hand-scrawled—became the core of a first-person narrative of life in the 1960s. In addition to providing a first-person account of coming of age in that tumultuous time, they weave together a story of deep and enduring friendships.

At first, I intended to simply publish the letters so that they would be preserved and shared. But it seemed as though a bit of context might be useful. Then one thing led to another.

The first part (chapters one through five) introduces the characters, the setting, and the social and political environment. The second part (chapters six through twelve) consists in large part of letters exchanged during our college years. The letters have been edited for brevity, but are otherwise presented as written. All the events described in the book actually happened, and all of the characters are real.

Prologue

I turned my head just as Jay began his free fall into space. We had just ushered him up the steps to the living room in Cooper's house where we were having the first gathering of the five us—Jay, Larry, Cooper, Bob and me—in almost 50 years. Instead of advancing into the room, Jay was falling backward.

Time, which makes all things possible then annihilates them one by one, had had its way. Gray-haired. Balding. Thick around the middle. We were no longer the gallant young lads we imagined ourselves to be.

Time had been particularly cruel to Jay. Parkinson's had robbed him of his strength and balance. He could no more arrest his fall than a slatted fence could hold back the tide.

Thump!
Thump!
Thump!
Thump!
Thump!

I saw his head and shoulders bounce on each of the stairs. There was a sickening thud when he hit the landing.

Holy Shit. I've killed him.

I hoped it wasn't so. We had planned to spend the day recounting stories and lies about growing up together in the 60s, I couldn't help but think: *this is gonna put a helluva damper on the reunion.*

Chapter 1

On the first Saturday in January, at the start of the new decade, I stood with my brother and sisters in the back of the Senate Caucus room, awaiting the arrival of the junior senator from Massachusetts.

The day had begun normally enough. I was wakened by the *Triumphal March* from *Aida* blaring from the stereo. Cranking up the volume was Dad's way of greeting the weekend. There was a shout from the kitchen where he was preparing scrambled eggs and toast. "Breakfast is ready." Just as we sat down, he said, "Eat up. We're leaving in twenty minutes." Then Mom sent us scurrying for clothes suitable for a trip to the city.

We piled into the family car—a white Comet Falcon—and sped down Colesville Road through Silver Spring. Dad calibrated his speed so he could roll through intersections just as the lights turned green.

Yesterday's snowfall had already turned into a gray, gritty slush that splattered onto the sidewalks and sent pedestrians scurrying as we sped by.

"Where we are going?" Dick asked.

"The Capitol," Dad said tersely.

I settled into the back seat, already uncomfortable in my starched shirt and checkerboard tie. Mary, a senior in high school, was buried in a book. The cover said *Jane Eyre*, but I had a hunch it was really *Peyton Place*. Kathy, at 10, the youngest, was crammed between the two of us, and Dick, 15, rode shotgun, the prerogative of the eldest son.

I glanced at my father. He was absorbed in the classical music playing on the radio. So far so good. Dad was at times quick to anger, especially if he thought he might be late. It paid to read his moods. He turned to Dick. "Did you bring a book?"

"Yeah," Dick answered, as if it were an option not to.

"What are you reading?"

"*The Jungle*—Upton Sinclair," Dick answered.

"Good book. You know he was one of the pioneers of muckraking journalism?"

"Yes, we talked about it in class."

"Are you a muckraker, Dad?" I asked.

"I don't really rake it," he responded, "but in this town there are times when I have to wade through it."

Crossing East-West highway, Dad turned up 16th Street. We passed the stately brick homes owned by Washington's elite. It was the route we travelled whenever we were dragooned into an excursion to a museum, a concert or a play. It was my father's favorite form of torture. I would have rather been at home listening to Hit Parade on my transistor radio (Bobby Darin's *Mack the Knife* was at the top of the charts) or reading a book. (I had just started to read Dick's copy of *Catcher in the Rye* —the one with Holden Caulfield pictured on the cover, standing in front of a strip joint and wearing a hunting cap. I had assumed that it was about baseball.)

Dad pulled the Comet into a parking lot.

"Let's go," Dad said as soon as we got out of the car.

We climbed the steps to the Senate Office Building, entered through brass-plated doors, and hurried down the hallway past the offices of senators and their staffs. I could hear the clatter of our footsteps on the marble floor as we raced to keep up with Dad. He always walked fast—a habit formed from years of working on deadline.

My father was a reporter for the Washington Daily News, the city's third largest newspaper after the Post and the Evening Star. When he wasn't at the News' headquarters, he was at the Capitol, covering Congress. He had taken us there lots of times. But it was odd to be there on a Saturday when Congress wasn't in session. Following hard behind him, we entered the Caucus Room. He directed us toward the back of the chamber, then he crowded his way to the front.

After a while, the din of conversation dissipated as a tall, slender Senator with movie star looks entered the room. He stood behind an array of microphones, and in a calm but forceful voice, he spoke: "I am announcing today my candidacy for the Presidency of the United States." He paused for effect, then continued.

> *The most important decisions of the century will be made over the next four years. Decisions about how to end the arms race; about how to support developing nations, and how to sustain our cities, our farms, our economy. Based on these issues the American people have to make a fateful choice. I have an image of America as a defender of freedom at this time of maximum peril and of the American people as confident, courageous and persevering. It is with this image that I begin this campaign.*

Reporters fired questions. Kennedy answered with the charm that would soon enthrall a nation and inspire so many of us to think we could change the world.

On the way home, Mary asked, "Do you think he will win?"

"Not a chance," Dad said.

Home Turf

I was born in 1947. I grew up in Silver Spring, a suburb of Washington D.C. After a week in the hospital, my mother and I came home to the house on Forest Glen Road that Dad had just purchased. It was a brick Tudor, with a tiny kitchen (much to my mother's annoyance), three bedrooms and a single bathroom. It also had an unfinished basement that was musty and dank, but it was affordable for a family living on a reporter's salary and only a short walk to Parkside Elementary School.

Our front yard was mostly taken up by a tall oak tree that smothered it in acorns each fall. There was room to play catch or ball or splash in an inflatable pool on a summer day. Our back yard was shaded by several maples onto which we tied ropes for swings and nailed boards to make a treehouse. We leveled a section of the yard so we could play basketball and badminton. Behind our lot was a large tract of untamed weeds, briars and vines. In spite of warnings about the perils of poison ivy, yellow jackets and black widow spiders, we spent hours exploring, digging tunnels and building forts. In the year of the locusts, we collected hundreds of specimens that we kept in jars under our beds until they died. A few years later, the land was bulldozed to build the Beltway.

My parents let us roam the neighborhood until dark. In summer, we walked or pedaled to the baseball field to play pick-up games. We ventured into woods, waded in creeks, and crawled through culverts. More than once, we found a box turtle and brought it home. We came back at midday for peanut butter and jelly sandwiches and chocolate milk, then went back out to play. Sometimes, Mom took us to the public pool to swim. Every so often, Dad took us to Griffith Stadium to watch the Washington Senators lose to the Yankees, or even worse, the reviled Baltimore Orioles.

Summers were hot and humid. To cool down, we ran through sprinklers and battled with water pistols. We rallied to the sound of the Good Humor truck bearing popsicles and ice cream bars. The evenings hummed with the sound of crickets. As darkness fell, we played capture the flag and chased fireflies. Sometimes we just lay on the grass looking at the stars. In the city, children played in the streets late into the night while mothers and fathers sat on porch stoops waiting for it to cool enough to sleep.

Silver Spring was becoming a sprawling commuter town. Government employment was steady, and the wages were high. One job could sustain a family. In the morning, white workers headed to the District while black men and women bussed to the suburbs to work at jobs that demanded long hours for little pay. In the process, enormous amounts of dollars flowed out of D.C. while bits of change trickled back in.

We had the best of both worlds. We lived in a serene setting just a few miles from the nation's capital, and we were able to take advantage of all that the city had to offer. We were forever exploring parks, museums and monuments: Mt. Vernon, the Lincoln and Jefferson Memorials, the Smithsonian, the Ford Theater, the White House, and the Library of Congress. We romped in Rock Creek Park, visited the zoo, and roamed the National Mall, where Dad sometimes played softball with other reporters and Congressmen. Best of all, Dad was able to get tickets to lots of concerts and plays. Our seats were always great. It made us feel like royalty.

The 1950s was the beginning of white flight spurred by racism and facilitated by the G.I. Bill and cheap gasoline. Neighborhoods that were successively home to WASPS, Eastern Europeans and Jews were abandoned in favor of surrounding towns. African-Americans who might also have chosen to leave the city were largely prevented from doing so by discriminative housing and lending practices. Soon, the majority of D.C. residents were black. Many were poor, but there was still a resilient core of entrepreneurs, lawyers, doctors, religious leaders, musicians and artists who sustained the city as a vibrant center of business, culture and political activism.

It seemed like everyone in my neighborhood was white. The students at Parkside Elementary were white. So were the teachers. Issues of race were not discussed in school. But by the beginning of the new decade, they were edging their way into our consciousness.

I grew up assuming that bigotry and segregation were confined to the Deep South. In reality, it infested Maryland as well. Although a part of the Union during the Civil War, slavery was not abolished in Maryland until a year after the Emancipation Proclamation. It was a Marylander, John Wilkes Booth, who assassinated President Lincoln. I don't recall seeing signs that said *Whites Only* or drinking fountains marked *Colored* where we lived, but many if not all local associations, neighborhoods and public facilities were segregated. At the end of sixth grade, Parkside Elementary sent all the safety patrols to Glen Echo Park. We were thrilled to have the run of the place, ride the roller coaster and gorge on cotton candy and other treats, the whole time oblivious to the fact that Negro children were barred from entering its gates.

Washington D.C. had always been a relatively safe harbor for African-Americans. But even into the 1960s, it offered no protection from discrimination. In many sections of the city, black people were not welcome. Restaurants and clubs catered to different races. The audiences at the National Theater, Constitution Hall, and Lisner Auditorium were white while black audiences patronized venues near 14th and U St. like the Lincoln and Howard Theaters, the Bohemian Caverns and the Velvet Lounge. Whites shopped at Woodward & Lothrup, Garfinkel's and Hecht's, while black shoppers were relegated to Sears, Morton's and Woolworths.

Racism also pervaded professional sports. When I was 10, I had a subscription to Sport Magazine which featured full-page photos of stars. I tacked one of Ted Kluzewski from the Cincinnati Reds, alarmingly muscular in his sleeveless jersey, on my bedroom wall. I loved Mickey Mantle and Yogi Berra from the Yankees, Luis Aparicio and Nellie Fox from the White Sox, and Mickey Vernon and Harmon Killebrew from the Nats. I idolized black athletes like Willie Mays and Hank Aaron, Jim Brown and Bobby Mitchell. But none played on my hometown teams. It wasn't until seven years after Jackie Robinson's debut, that Carlos Paula, a Cuban, became the first black player on the Washington Senators. He played only two seasons. When Calvin Griffith took over the team from his father in 1955, he refused to sign black players. When he moved the Senators to Minnesota in 1961, he said,

> *I'll tell you why we came to Minnesota. It was when we found out you only had 15,000 blacks here. Black people*

don't go to ballgames, but they'll fill up a rassling ring and put up such a chant it'll scare you to death. We came here because you've got good, hardworking white people here.

George Preston Marshall, owner of the Redskins, was no better. The reason he didn't have black players, he said, was because it would ruin the image of the Redskins as the "team of the American South." He also said, "We'll start signing Negroes when the Harlem Globetrotters start signing whites."

Marshall may never have integrated the team without pressure from the White House that came as the Redskins prepared to move into a new federally funded stadium. It probably didn't help that the American Nazi Party picketed outside of the stadium carrying signs that pleaded, "Keep Our Redskins White."

Marshall soon caved. After a one-win season, the team got the first pick in the 1961 draft and chose Ernie Davis—the first black Heisman Trophy winner. Davis refused to sign with the Redskins and was traded to the Browns for Bobby Mitchell. Fifteen years after the NFL color line was broken, the Redskins were integrated. It had been a long time coming.

The Specter of Annihilation

I was born two years after the end of World War II. The Korean War was over by the time I turned five. The biggest threats were the Soviet Union and, as Senator McCarthy avowed, from Communists within. To be sure, there was a succession of regional conflicts including the Hungarian Revolt, the Suez Crisis, and the revolution in Cuba, but they seemed a world away. Still, it was a scary time. The arms race between the U.S. and U.S.S.R. seemed to be a runaway train that no one could stop, and the possibility of nuclear war clawed at our consciousness.

Classes at Parkside were periodically interrupted by air raid drills. On hearing the siren, we were instructed to duck under our tiny wooden desks and cover our necks with our hands. This did little to allay our fears. We knew that once the bombs were dispatched, it would all be over in an instant. We had visions of people evaporating in a sudden blast of heat. Anyone living near Washington would be among the first to go. Talk of war was common, and mushroom clouds inhabited my dreams.

Some residents even built air raid shelters. While I was 13, my friend Nancy led me through a short passageway in her basement to an underground room. There were shelves of canned food and other supplies, a table and four chairs, four fold-out bunks, and a shelf full of classic literature including the *Swiss Family Robinson*. I heard the whirr of a fan that would bring in air for breathing. But how would that help if all the oxygen was sucked out of the sky? I asked her if there was a gun to keep the mobs out. She said she didn't know. Just thinking about it was scary. She held my hand tight as we made our retreat. She told me that her parents had told her that building the shelter would get rid of her nightmares, but it only made them worse.

The Soviet Union cast a dark shadow. It was us against them. The American way against godless communism. We were patriotic and celebrated the flag and the Fourth of July. At school, good behavior was rewarded with highly coveted Freedom Cards that meant you could go to the library or the garden on your own. I doubted they had such things in the U.S.S.R.

Chapter 2

Larry Horwitz

At the beginning of the 60s, I was in the 7th grade at Eastern Jr. High. It was a sprawling education factory with 1,000 students. I was on the precipice of puberty. Most boys in my class felt lucky to have a hint of pubic hair. The girls, on the other hand, were busting out all over.

Going from elementary school to junior high with its changing classes, army of teachers, and hallways lined with lockers was an important rite of passage. It made me feel like a grown-up. But it was also harrowing. Instead of being at the top of elementary school, I was part of the uncertain, stuttering class—much smaller than the towering, nearly bearded 9th graders, thrust into a clamor of boasts, putdowns and humiliations. I was a nervous wreck in the locker room, fearful of snapping towels and random shoves from older boys. The teachers were menacing. They assaulted us with homework and tormented us with pop quizzes. Complaints, eye-rolling, and backtalk were met by harsh glares, after-school detention, or a march to the principal's office.

The first day of seventh grade was particularly nerve-wracking. Wearing the clothes that I had just purchased at J.C. Penney and armed with a new three-ring binder, I reluctantly slouched out of the car. "Have a great day. Call me when you get home," Dad said as he pulled the car away. That was it. No words of advice to fortify me. I already longed to be back at Parkside.

I negotiated the labyrinth of hallways and found the section of the gym set aside for incoming students. I got a schedule, a locker number and lock, and proceeded to my homeroom. I did as I was told and spoke to no one. After three confusing classroom shifts, I entered the cafeteria. I hoped to find a fellow Parkside graduate, but no luck. I figured my choices were to sit by myself or hide in a bathroom stall. Instead I chucked the paper bag of food my mother had packed and exited through the back door. There, I ran into a motley crowd of odd-sized boys conversing furiously. One of them, Larry Horwitz, was holding forth in a booming voice. He was talking a mile a minute. The other boys were rapt as he peppered them with the facts of life in a monologue that was punctured by bursts of laughter—mostly his own—that could be heard three counties away.

I was no expert, but it struck me that much of what he said was made up, especially what he said about the rhythm method. "It's something that Catholics like to do—you know—giving her the old one-and-a-two-and-a-three."

I couldn't stay silent. "The rhythm method doesn't really work you know."

"Of course, it doesn't work," he exclaimed. "Have you ever seen a Catholic family? They always have a dozen kids."

"My mom says spermicidal jelly works the best." (*Oh crap...had I really just said the word mom?*) "She works for Planned Parenthood," I added.

"Jelly! What do you do? Spread it on toast?"

"On the vagina," I said. I knew this much only because we sometimes encountered cardboard boxes labeled Vaginal Jelly in the hallway at home.

"Yeah?" he said. "Well, my father uses rubbers."

All I could think of were the shiny black galoshes my parents made me wear on rainy days when I walked to school. Fortunately the bell rang before the limits of my knowledge were further tested, and everyone scrambled inside.

That night, I decided to improve my command of certain terms before I went back to school. I counted on my mother to be a trustworthy source. We could ask her or tell her anything. Plus, she was passionate about anything to do with birth control. It was just one of her causes. Soon after we moved to Silver Spring, she met other mothers who were also well-educated, well-read, and politically engaged. Together they created a co-op pre-school. Later on, she became active in the PTA, the League of Women Voters, and the Democratic Party.

As a former journalist herself, she often designed the brochure, published the newsletter or sent out press releases for whatever cause she was involved in. Now she was doing it for Planned Parenthood. That's how my baby picture ended up in a pamphlet about prophylactics.

"Mom," I asked when we were alone, "what exactly is the rhythm method?"

"Well," she said. "Maybe I should start at the beginning." She then gave a synopsis of human sexuality. By the end, she had undone much of the confusion that was caused by an uncomfortable hour spent in elementary school watching a sex education film. The film, I recalled, consisted mostly of a recitation of Latin terms for certain body parts and complicated diagrams that looked a lot like Chutes and Ladders. It had left me bewildered.

The next day I saw Larry in the back of my math class. If he was expecting to go unnoticed, it wasn't working. There was no way he could stay silent. He was glib, jokey and short on impulse control. He entertained the students and drove the teachers to despair. As I was soon to learn and appreciate, he was indefatigably ebullient, unabashed and prone to exaggeration—in other words, a budding raconteur. Larry had a habit of turning every incident into a story, and every story became apocryphal. For my own part, I was more of an observer—most comfortable as a witness. I threw in a wry comment here and there, but mostly I listened.

Soon we became best friends. It wasn't long before I was spending almost as much time at Larry's house as I did at my own. Larry's parents, Buddy and Gloria, told great stories as well. I liked them especially because they were so different from my own. They were effusive and profane. Mine were reserved and proper. At our house, decorum prevailed. At Larry's, chaos ensued.

His father, Buddy, was particularly fascinating. He appeared to have many different jobs. The most constant one was delivering legal papers to scofflaws and debt dodgers. He umpired softball games on the weekends for extra money. He also was quite the football fan. Sometimes I came over to their house on a Sunday to watch the Redskins. Buddy spent the whole time barking into a telephone and sweating profusely. Only later did I realize he was taking bets.

The Horwitz residence was a great diversion. I was entertained by the endless squabbles involving their three sons (Larry, Jack and David). I was mesmerized by the high drama that erupted without warning. Stuff happened there that simply never did at my house. One night, when we were still in seventh grade, Larry announced before dinner, "God I'm feeling horny tonight."

Buddy laughed. "Do you know what that means, Larry?"

"Of course, I do," Larry responded. "It means I'm so hungry I could eat a horse."

When we were in high school, Buddy treated us like peers. He let us smoke. (At my house, we were barely allowed to chew gum). He told dirty jokes. He mocked us for being virgins but, at the same time, he tried to help us in his way.

"If you are not too chicken shit," he said, "I know a woman named Rita on V Street who will fix you up."

"You're not serious," Larry said.

"Sure. If you have the balls to go down there, I'll give you her address."

The next Friday night, five of us piled in Jay's white Chrysler and headed into D.C. We were full of raucous bravado which ebbed precipitously as we got closer. As we pulled up to the house, I felt like I was about to break out in hives.

We all turned to Larry. "Go in and find out what the deal is," Jay said.

"We'll all go," Larry said.

"Of course, we will," Jay said. "But you go first."

Larry got out of the car. We watched him slowly ascend the steps and knock on the door. An older man answered it. He stared incredulously.

"We're here to see Rita." Larry said.

"Rita? What the hell are you talking about? There ain't no Rita here."

Larry apologized profusely, then nearly jumped off the porch in his haste to get back in the car.

"Sorry boys," Larry announced. "There ain't no Rita here."

Jay fired up the Chrysler and took off right away, much to our relief.

"Well," said Larry. "It'll make for a good story."

Jay Levy

After a few months in the 7th grade, I joined an intramural basketball team. We didn't have any great players but there was a kid named Jay Levy who was taller than everyone else.

"Stay under the basket and I'll get you the ball," I said.

Whenever I got the ball, I looped it to him, and he put it up for a score. Soon we were destroying the competition. But on the day of the championship game, Jay was nowhere to be seen. He later insisted that he had to stay home that day because he'd cut his finger. I was bitter with disappointment. *What a flake*, I thought.

Nevertheless, we became friends. He lived a few blocks from the school, and I stopped on my way home to eat snacks and listen to music. Jay had a record player in his room and a stack of 45s. After we went through a few of those, he put on a Tito Puente album that blasted out a torrent of sounds played with rhythmic fury. "It's my dad's dance music," Jay told me.

As much as his eclectic taste in music surprised me, I was shocked by what came next. We went into his living room where there was a shiny spinet piano. "Listen to this." He sat down, and began to play like a pro. It was a mystery. He seemed to be able to reproduce whatever melody he heard. I was used to seeing my father labor long to master a single piece on the piano, but here he was, without the benefit of proper lessons or even sheet music, zipping through the hit parade.

When he was eight, Jay's cousin showed him how to pick out *In the Mood* on the piano. Afterward, he went home and played until he mastered it. Then he began rifling through his father's collection of big band and swing music, Broadway shows, and the Cuban music to play. By age ten, he was gulping down the hydrant flow of hits on the AM radio stations—songs by early rockers like Elvis, Chuck Berry, Carl Perkins and Fats Domino.

I don't know how many times I listened as he pounded out *What'd I Say*, like a young, Jewish Ray Charles. Or we'd go to parties where he entertained by playing songs like *Runaway* by Del Shannon, *Please Mr. Postman* by the Marvelettes, or one by Frankie Ford:

Oo-ee, oo-ee baby,
Oo-ee, oo-ee baby,
Oo-ee, oo-ee baby,
Won't ya let me take you on a sea cruise.

Jay loved coming over to my house where we combed through the floor-to-ceiling shelves filled with albums that record companies had sent to Dad in hope he would review them in the paper. Most were classical, but there was also plenty of jazz.

Jay knew jazz from the inside out. He understood how it was built on key changes, chord progressions, and time signatures. All of that was a mystery to me. I knew just enough to lose myself in it. Listening took me to a place where everyone was speaking a language I didn't know but somehow understood. We listened for hours to LPs that grew scratchy with use. *Miles Ahead. Time Out. Mingus Ah Um. Waltz for Debby.*

Monk's Dream. They were the slow trains that transported us from the humdrum to the exotic—New Orleans, Chicago, Memphis and New York City.

After school, we went to the new library on Colesville Road to read the latest issue of *Down Beat*. In a car, we'd listen to the jazz station and try to name who was playing.

"That's Miles," one of us would say, on first hearing his unmistakable sound.

"Obviously."

"What track?"

"*So What*."

"But who's on bass?"

That was harder. "Ron Carter?"

In addition to his musical precocity, there were lots of reasons to look up to Jay. He was tall, handsome and sartorial. He wore real Bass Weejun loafers and Brooks Brother's shirts, neither of which could be found at JC Penney. He was funny, fearless and unpredictable. In time, Jay became the anchor of our crew—the first one up for an adventure and the last one to leave. Sometimes, after the rest of us had gone to bed, he would stand outside of Larry's house tossing rocks at his window, because he wasn't ready to call it a night. Jay grew up the fastest. He was the first to have a steady, long-term girlfriend, and we were pretty sure that they were constantly having sex. But that didn't keep him from other amorous encounters. At least that's what we believed.

Bernard Cooper

I didn't meet Cooper until the eighth grade. Once I did, I found him to be endlessly interesting. Tall and angular, he would swoop in at unexpected moments and make an esoteric remark or wry comment. Then he would disappear. As time went on, he was always a part of, but never constrained by, the pack. He was a free spirit with a knack for skirting rules.

It was about that time that we started hanging out in the business district in Silver Spring. On Saturdays, we'd go there to meet up with friends from school. If we were lucky, we'd run into girls we knew and join the mobs of teenagers flowing from one store to the next for no particular purpose, or packing the booths at Hot Shoppes.

Sometimes, we would go see a movie at the Silver Theater, notable for its Art Deco façade, or cull through books at Brentano's or 45s at Variety Records where you could listen to records in a sound booth without having to buy them.

If we ran into Cooper, we might spend hours playing pinball machines, pumping in nickels, refining our flipper skills, and mastering the art of lifting the machine just enough to guide the silvery steel balls without tilting. We competed to get a high score and win free plays. We played at the bowling alley or in the back of the smoke shop on Fenton Avenue, where we could play for free.

"Keep your eye on the guy behind the counter," Cooper said.

"All clear," I mouthed.

Cooper inserted a key into a small metal door in the back of the machine. With a flip of the switch, he racked up about 30 free games. It made for a great afternoon.

While the oversight of my parents tended to keep me on the straight and narrow, Cooper and Levy were less encumbered. So it was that the two of them took three buses into the heart of the city to some denizen who was supplying the suburbs with illegal firecrackers—cherry bombs, ashcans, and M-80s. As soon as they got back, they ignited their armaments in the street in front of Jay's house, turning the quiet suburban block into a scene out of *Back to Bataan*. A neighbor reported them right away. When they heard the police coming, Cooper hightailed it home through a series of back yards and alley ways. Jay ran into his house. While the cops pounded on his door, he hid under his bed.

"You should have been there when we put that cherry bomb in the trash can," Jay said when I saw him next. "It blew the lid sky high."

Cooper was the first one to hitchhike. He started when he was in the fifth grade, and sometimes journeyed far beyond the state line. He imparted his skills to the rest of us.

"Never tell a driver where you're going," he said. "Just ask him if he's going straight. What can he say but yes? That's when you hop in." We all took it up, and it made it easy to get around. From about the eighth grade to the tenth, we went everywhere by thumb.

While Jay and I were listening to jazz, Cooper was unearthing folk music, blues and bluegrass. Sometimes I'd go to his house, and he would cue up his Teac reel-to-reel tape player. We listened to Alan Lomax recordings of old musicians playing on weather-beaten porch steps in Appalachia or the Mississippi Delta. It was at Cooper's house that I first heard of Lester Flatt and Earl Scruggs, Woodie Guthrie, Leadbelly and Howlin' Wolf. Once in a while, he showed me the progress he was making learning to play slide guitar.

During high school, he was usually off on his own or with some beatnik friends. They frequented places in D.C. with names like *Coffee and Confusion*, the *Open Way*, and the *Live Eye*, where caffeine was the drug of choice. Cooper had the impression that if he got to know the right people, pot was to be had. At least that was his hope.

Bob Ochsman
Bob went to Montgomery Junior High (we called it Monkey High), so I didn't meet him until I was halfway through the eighth grade. He quickly meshed with our group. He shared our interests in girls, music, and cars.

In the suburbs, cars were king. As kids, we made model cars, gluing them together, painting them and adding flame decals behind the wheels. We went to auto shows, memorized makes and models, and argued long over which ones would merit our ownership once we got older. Bob and Jay were obsessed with fast cars. They both had a head for engine displacements, horsepower and gear ratios. Neither could wait to get his drivers' license. In fact, they were driving even before they got learners' permits. This put them on a collision course with the Montgomery County police, and earned them a cameo in the Washington Post.

In the ninth grade, Jay and Bob nefariously obtained a set of General Motors master keys. In the evenings, at times well beyond my curfew, they roamed the streets until they came upon a late model Chevy or Buick or Oldsmobile that they borrowed for a ride. Miraculously they managed to return the cars unscathed somewhere close to where they had stolen them. They continued these capers even after one of their running buddies was sent up to the Lorton Detention Center. But it all came to a halt one afternoon when the two were at Bob's house, and Bob's father, Vic, entered the room.

"Boys, let's go for a ride." Bob and Jay looked nervously at each other. Vic was not known to make casual offers. Levy climbed into the back seat. As usual, he was carrying his purloined keys because, he said, "You never know if you're going to need a ride." After settling into the back seat, Jay shoved the keys into the crack between the cushions. Vic took them right to the police station, where they were interrogated in separate rooms.

"We cracked immediately," Bob reported. "But we got off with probation, and the story made it into the newspaper. All in all, it was a pretty good deal."

Bob's whole family was car crazy. His parents drove a Lincoln Continental convertible. It had suicide doors that swung outward, and it was the size of a cruise ship. It was also a rare model, so it was no surprise that the White House asked Vic to use the car to transport the new president and first lady in the Inaugural Parade, which, of course, he let them do. Bob's brother had a silver Corvette that he lent to Bob on rare occasions, and Bob had a bronze Mustang—one of the first —that his Dad gave him when he turned sixteen.

Bob rounded out our group. He was the most studious. That is to say, he took school seriously. He was curious about the world and how things worked, and did his homework. I appreciated that about him. He was good in math and science. Neither held much interest for me. Mostly I just wanted to read books and write stories. I supposed that Bob's parents, like mine, must have expected their children to do well in school and go off to a good college.

Those were my pals, my mates, my brothers: Larry, Jay, Cooper and Bob. From junior high on, we shared a dizzying series of trials, tribulations and misadventures.

Chapter 3

Call to Duty

JFK's inauguration fell on a brilliant sunny day in January 1961, when the temperature was in the 20s. Thousands of citizens assembled to see him sworn in. It had snowed the night before. The bare branches of trees around the Mall gleamed in the sunlight. The ground was covered with snow. The streets and parking lots were glazed with ice. The Capitol and all the storied buildings nearby looked pristine and blameless.

Our family sat in the press section in front of the Capitol steps. We were snug in wool coats and hats and scarves, but the wait was long. To keep from freezing, we stamped our feet and rubbed our hands. We were near the stage, and had a close-up view of President-elect Kennedy, Jacqueline Kennedy, Chief Justice Warren, President Lyndon and Lady Bird Johnson and other luminaries. Behind us stretched a sea of spectators, while millions more watched from home.

The inauguration began with a prayer. Marian Anderson sang *The Star Spangled Banner*. An 87 year-old Robert Frost had written a poem entitled *Dedication* for the occasion, but because of the sun's glare, he could barely see the words. He put it aside and recited *The Gift Outright*. Hatless in the cold, Kennedy spoke in soaring tones, "The torch has been passed to a new generation of Americans" and he demanded, "Ask not what your country can do for you. Ask what you can do for your country."

The contrast between the Kennedys and the outgoing President and First Lady Mamie Eisenhower was stark. The Eisenhowers were from an earlier generation. The Kennedys were young, charismatic and irresistible. It felt like a new era had begun. It was the first day of Camelot—that perfect place that we thought would last forever.

The decade of the 60s began with great hope, but dark clouds were massing. The Soviets were a growing threat. The struggle for civil rights was erupting, and long-standing political coalitions were about to be reshuffled. Still, we had a promising leader, a man of vision and grace, whom we were ready to follow, and a country we were anxious to serve.

The Awakening

At Eastern Junior High, I was doing my best to navigate the complex, opaque and semi-libidinous world of teenagers. I discovered girls and found them to be eye-turning, funny, and intriguing. I fell asleep each night awash with confusion and desire, as I contemplated the mysteries of their quickly maturing bodies and feminine charms. Such thoughts were stirred by sock-hops at school where we jitterbugged to the music of the Coasters, Frankie Avalon and the Everly Brothers, and chaperoned parties where we danced cheek to hot-flushed cheek.

During the eighth grade, Larry, Jay and I joined a Jewish fraternity called AZA which held frequent socials with its sorority counterpart, B'nai B'rith Girls. Through AZA, I learned to play poker from Carl Bernstein who was more than happy to clean out our wallets. A few years later, after he dropped out of college to become a reporter, Carl told Larry that he could get him a job at the Washington Post. "Nah," Larry said. "I'm going to stick with college. You can't get anywhere without a degree."

I might have been the only *goy* in AZA but I didn't think of it as odd. Most of the kids I was closest to were Jewish, and part of what seemed like an inner circle of people named Goldberg, Weinstein, Levy and Cohen. They had intimate knowledge of exotic foods (*corned beef and pastrami, matzo ball soup, knishes and latkes, chopped chicken liver!*), and participated in a variety of rituals that were solemn and mysterious.

At least I was part Jewish. My grandfather, Louis, was an Orthodox Jew who immigrated to America from Europe as a teenager. My father was raised Jewish, but our family was not religious. My mother was descended from a long line of Protestant ministers (the Smythes and the Bulkleys) that went back to the early colonialists, but she was not particularly interested in organized religion. She took us to a Congregational church for the purpose of our cultural edification, but the only one who took to it was my brother Dick who became a Methodist. We celebrated Christmas and Easter. On Christmas Eve, we went to see the giant Christmas tree on the Mall which the President lit up with a switch in the White House. When we got home, we hung stockings. Dad played the piano, and we sang Christmas carols. But Christmas was more about the lights, the music, and presents than anything else.

That said, I spent a good number of Saturday mornings in nearby synagogues attending my friends' Bar Mitzvahs. Personally, I thought they were classic examples of wishful thinking. While we were experiencing bodily changes, cracking voices, and hormonal chaos, we were a long way from manhood. It made the ceremonies seem at least five years premature.

Bar Mitzvahs began with a fairly solemn Saturday morning service in which my friends would demonstrate their hard won proficiency in Hebrew by reading from the Torah from right to left. Then they would deliver thoughtful, even witty and philosophical observations on the lessons they learned from their rabbi. I felt humbled watching them perform. The service was followed by a brunch featuring bagels, cream cheese and lox, gefilte fish, pickled herring, Danish pastries and other delights. By evening, my friends, to my relief, reverted from their just celebrated maturity to their inane selves in time for the party to begin. There were always lots of friends and family, young boys in sport coats and ties, and girls in party dresses, music and dancing, food and drink. I particularly appreciated how the inebriated grown-ups left half-finished screwdrivers abandoned on tables. The drinks were fair game. It was at these parties that I had my first taste of drunkenness and the nausea that ensued.

About this time, friends became paramount, and I would do anything to get out of the house. I was increasingly annoyed by my parents' relentless concern for my well-being. If I stayed home, Dad would inevitably hound me to clean my room or do my homework. It seemed so unfair. The only way to avoid it was to be buried in a book. But as much as I liked to read, I wanted nothing more than to be with friends, and Silver Spring was a great place to meet up.

On a day off from school in February, I left early to take advantage of the Washington's Birthday Sales. Larry and I got there when the stores first opened, and stayed the rest of the day. Somehow, the hours drifted away. It was dark before I knew it. I hadn't bothered to tell my parents where I was going. By now, Dad would be anxious and furious, and my mother would be entreating the gods for me to call.

Dad confronted me as soon as I walked in the door. "Where in God's name have you been and what have you been doing?"

"Silver Spring. Nothing much." *What else was there to say?*

"Really? I want you to write down everything you did from the start of the day until you got home"

I was sent to my room and told not to come out until I provided a full accounting of the day. Two hours later, groggy with exhaustion, I emerged from my room with seven hand-scrawled pages that began:

> *It was a wintry February morn. But even before dawn's first light sun broke sharply on the rain-glazed streets of the city, he was up and dressed. Stealthily, he exited the house, taking the first few steps on what would be a harrowing mission. He would not return without accomplishing it, no matter the cost...*

It went on from there in gothic tones until the ending.

...Wearily, he trudged the last mile over feckless fields toward home. Gasping what might be his last breath, he fell, his body and spirit depleted, over the welcome threshold that led to hearth and home.

Dad placed the sheets of paper on the dining room table and took out a red pencil. As he read through them, he furiously added commas, crossed ts, circled misspellings, and pitilessly excised any word or phrase he deemed unnecessary.

He handed them back to me. The red pencil marks were everywhere. It looked like a top secret document that had been redacted before release.

"You are off the hook for now. But don't disappear like that again."

Then, after a pause, he said, "You know, with a bit of effort, you could become a writer someday."

"Thank you," I said stonily. Inside I was beaming.

Montgomery Blair High School
My high school was the size of New Delhi. Sprawling. Immense. Crowded. It was a great place for achievers, math geniuses, alpha athletes, budding stars and pageant winners. It was also an easy place to feel overlooked, invisible or lost. But it was big enough that everyone, whether an egghead, jock, greaser, poet or artist, malcontent, joiner or lone wolf—could eventually find some sympathetic souls with whom to consort.

The school was located beside the sylvan, rocky Sligo Creek Park. The student body, which numbered nearly 3,000, was white with the exception of the sons or daughters of foreign diplomats and perhaps a dozen or so Negro students. The faculty was only slightly more diverse than the student body. There were no gay people—at least who were acknowledged. There were Catholics, Protestants, and Jews, but I wasn't aware of any Muslims, Buddhists, or Sikhs.

Slogging through school was an ordeal. Too many abysmal classes, indifferent teachers, rote assignments and long days interrupted by rare moments of insight, epiphany and joy which usually occurred outside of class.

Larry ended up at Northwood High School, but the rest of us went to Blair. There we expanded our circle to include characters like Tommy (Mad Dog) Howell. He was an artist of sorts. Once I asked him what he was working on. "The History of Electricity in Wet Fresco," he replied.

Eric Barslaag was another creative sort who once cut a hole in a canvas, put it over his head and spun it around his neck. He got a B minus.

Walter Mitchell went to class irregularly at best and did a minimal amount of work. In his junior year, he decided to mess with people's minds by getting straight A's. His parents and teachers were astounded and thrilled. But the next term, he reverted to form and squeaked by with Ds.

Alvin Rothman never asked or responded to a question in our French class. Nor did he turn in any assignments. He just sat quietly in the back of the room reading Dostoyevsky's *The Idiot*.

I found these and many others to be interesting, irreverent and sometimes dangerous--exactly what I needed to offset my own inclination to fit in and get along. I had way too much *what would my parents say* going on my head, while these guys were mostly thinking *why the fuck not?*

Wheels

Becoming old enough to drive was life-altering. I took my driving test the day after my 16th birthday. I managed to finesse the parallel parking and pass. But as soon as the examiner exited the car, I made an illegal U-turn across three lanes of traffic. I glimpsed him waving his fist at me in the rear view mirror as I pulled away.

Having a license made for an ever-widening circle of exploration. Like most teenagers, we were unworthy of the trust placed in us by the powers that allowed brainless, irresponsible children to get behind a wheel.

Jay had regular access to his father's powerful, white Chrysler. It had wide bench seats which could hold six or more. Sometimes, after downing a few beers, he would get on the Beltway and coax the car to 100 mph. It never failed to terrify.

Bob was zipping around town in his Mustang. Larry occasionally wrested his father's Ford Galaxy. I had to share our family's one car with my parents and brother. At least Mary was already in college, and Kathy was too young to drive. There was never any status in driving the family car. Dad was sure to buy the bare bones model. Our Chevy Biscayne had neither air conditioning nor power steering. It was so stripped down that most of the dashboard dials were blank.

It felt like we spent the better part of our lives in or around cars. Friday and Saturday nights consisted of driving up and down Colesville Road, Georgia Avenue and East-West Highway or winding it out on the road to Damascus where the Ochsmans had a small farm.

We were occasionally challenged by other young drivers to see who could lay down the most rubber coming off a green light. Often the contests were preceded by various taunts:

Daddy's car.
Trailer trash.
Fucking kike.

"What I don't get," Jay pondered "is how they know I'm Jewish?"

"They don't, Jay," I told him. "They call everybody a kike."

Now mobile, we could search far and wide for girls, parties, and thrills. We could stop for 15 cent hamburgers at McDonald's or pull into Hot Shoppes where we ordered Mighty Mos and onion rings that were delivered to our car on a tray.

Sometimes we ventured to nightspots in D.C. Although we were still under the legal drinking age (18), we talked our way into jazz clubs like the Bohemian Caverns and Cellar Door to see Dizzy Gillespie, Thelonious Monk and Charlie Byrd. Or we'd go to jazz joints on 14th St. to see less celebrated but still mesmerizing musicians. At times we were the only white people in the place.

"You know you boys could get jumped and rolled down here," one black hipster explained to me while I was in the john after downing a couple of beers.

"True enough," I said. "But it's the only place that'll serve us."

"I can dig it," he said.

Road trips beckoned. One February morning, Larry, Cooper, Bob and I hopped into Jay's Chrysler. Instead of going to school, we headed up the New Jersey Turnpike on a mission to secure jobs in the Catskills for the coming summer. As soon as we got to New York, we made a beeline to an employment office called Dependable Harold's somewhere on the lower East Side. We crowded into his tiny office. The walls were plastered with outdated want ads and pictures from exotic locales.

Five steps from the front door was a heavy maple desk, smothered by application forms and hastily scrawled notes, a beat up typewriter and a rotary phone. Sitting behind the desk was Harold, wearing a green eyeshade. He had a goiter on his neck the size of a peach.

"We're here to get summer jobs," Larry said. "In the Catskills. I'm thinking Grossinger's. What do you got?"

"You're three months early boys."

"Well, we came a long way so I don't know when we could come back. We wanted to get a jump on it."

"Come back in May," he said and waved goodbye.

What a disaster, I thought.

"For chrissakes, Larry" I said when we were out on the sidewalk. "Why didn't you find that out before we came all the way here?"

"Fuck you, Berliner. Would you rather be sitting in history class? Don't you get it? We're here on a lark. A fucking lark!"

We spent the day roaming Manhattan. I had been before to visit my grandparents, but this was the first time on my own. It was cool to be in places I knew from books and movies. We wandered everywhere, dodging traffic, digging the cacophony of voices, horns and sirens, gawking at the Empire State Building, and eating greasy slices of pizza. We walked in circles inside the Guggenheim Museum amid the modern masterpieces. We loitered in Washington Square and combed Greenwich Village in search of Ernie's Bar so we could order a few cocktails just like Holden Caulfield. Then we figured out that the bar, like the book, was fictional.

At about six, we climbed into the Chrysler, waded into the traffic and drove through the Holland Tunnel and onto the freeway. We didn't get home until after ten. Fortunately, I had thought to call home earlier to say I might be late for dinner.

"Where were you all this time?" my mother asked when I got back.

"With the guys." I said, "Studying for a test."

Jay usually captained these epic journeys, first in the white Chrysler and later in a teal blue Chevy Impala convertible with the 360 horsepower engine that he convinced his parents they needed. But what he wanted most was a car of his own. That was rectified, at least for a time, after a surprising call from Walter Mitchell.

"Jay, my mom says we're moving to Hawaii."

"Whaaaat?"

"Yeah Hawaii. Would you mind taking care of the car while I'm gone?"

"Does the Pope have testicles?" Jay responded.

It was a jet black 1957 Chrysler 300 C with a 375 hp hemi engine and a Torque-Flite, three-speed automatic pushbutton transmission. It was a drag racing machine. Jay was over the moon. The Saturday after Mitchell turned the car over to him, Jay and Bob took it up Route 75 to the raceway in Manassas. On arriving, they removed the hood to lighten the car. Then

Jay crawled underneath and disconnected the exhaust from the manifold so that it sounded even nastier.

"We definitely got respect," Bob reported.

The 300C offered new opportunities for hot-rodding, which Jay did for several months until the engine blew up.

Jay, having no previous mechanical experience, decided to rebuild the engine himself. He had his own torque wrench. What could possibly go wrong?

Bob generously offered his garage to use while his family went to Florida for the holidays. Jay coaxed the crippled heap across town, the engine clanking like a jail house door the entire way. He spent the next week unbolting whatever he could until he realized he would need an engine hoist to disconnect the transmission. "Hell, I didn't even have a creeper," Jay explained.

Days later, the engine was still in pieces on the garage floor as they were heading home from Florida. Jay hastily swept them up and crammed them into the trunk. He pushed the Chrysler onto the street just minutes before they arrived.

"It sat there two months," Bob said. "My father asked me every fucking day when Jay was going to get it out of there." Eventually, Jay had it towed to a garage and had the engine professionally rebuilt. "It cost me an arm and a leg, but it ran like a dream."

Chapter 4

The March on Washington

Television, from the fifties onward, crept insidiously into our lives. It irritated Dad to no end when television crews muscled their way into Senate hearings and blocked the view of the print reporters with their clunky cameras, cables and lights.

Televisions were pricey. We had to make do with a black-and-white Motorola with weak reception and a touchy vertical hold. We were restricted to watching one show a night, plus Sunday telecasts of the Redskins. Leonard Bernstein's *Young People's Concerts* were mandatory, and on Sundays we watched Steve Allen or Ed Sullivan.

The power of television to command the attention of the nation was manifest as stations began to cover the sit-ins in Greensboro, North Carolina in 1961. Four black college students sat at a segregated lunch counter and refused to leave until they were served. White patrons heckled, threatened and spewed hate, but the demonstrators refused to budge. The next day, more students joined in. Woolworth's capitulated. Other demonstrations followed. From then on, we were deluged by images of protestors, many of them teenagers, taunted by bigots, bloodied by police, and hauled to jail.

It felt both immediate yet removed. In spite of the urgency of the headlines, I lived in a world in which my most pressing concerns were what to wear, how to get a date, and whether the incipient pimple on the side of my nose would be the final blow to my shaky self-esteem.

In September 1962, James Meredith, with the aid of 500 U.S. Marshals, became the first African-American student at the University of Mississippi. The following year, Governor Wallace tried to block the doors of the University of Alabama to keep black students from entering, and the horrifying scenes of fire hoses and dogs turned against lawful protesters leapt out from our tv.

By the summer of 1963, President Kennedy's hand was forced. On June 11, he took to the airwaves to call for Congressional action. His speech raised hopes, but they were punctured just four hours later when Medgar Evers, a veteran civil rights worker, was shot in the back after coming home from an organizing meeting at a nearby church.

On August 28th, after months of planning, a quarter of a million people convened in Washington D.C. for the March on Washington for Jobs and Freedom. It was a beautiful day. Traffic was light because so many people were afraid to go downtown. Dad, as a journalist, did not participate, but he did chauffeur my sister Mary and me to the March. As we walked the final blocks to the Mall, we could see a river of chartered buses arriving from New York, Vermont, Illinois and other states. At least one bus came all the way from California.

The roads leading to the Mall were jammed with people, old and young. The marchers were polite and well-dressed. Many of the men wore coats and ties. The women, dresses or skirts. The vast majority of the marchers were African-American, but there was a strong showing of white people as well.

Some groups wore matching hats or vests decorated with buttons or carried signs with slogans like *Equal Rights Now! Civil Rights Plus Full Employment,* and *No Dough to Help Jim Crow.* An NAACP contingent from Philadelphia wore black denim whalers with their names printed on the back. Everyone was friendly. We spent the hours sitting on the grass in the shade of elms, eating popsicles, talking, laughing and trying to absorb the moment. There were interesting people to observe and enjoy, and many young women and girls to admire. Various delegations passed by. A young man—a boy really—started singing *"Ain't gonna let Jim Crow turn me around."* Everyone joined in. I felt immersed in a sea of hope. Change was just around the corner. It just had to be.

At times it felt more like a picnic than a protest. But not everyone saw it that way. The idea of tens of thousands of Negroes supported by large numbers of white people who were probably communists or worse, scared the hell out of a lot of people. The President ordered troops to stand ready just in case.

After a few hours, the speeches began. A man at the podium said he had just roller-skated to Washington from Chicago, and that his legs were pretty tired. Could one more person really make a difference? I was glad that I came, if only to be counted. All around me were people whose skin was a shade of brown. It was not what I had ever experienced before. I was acutely aware of the color of my skin which was not only white but frightfully pale. Even after months of summer, I wasn't even tan—more a freckled reddish-pink. I wished I was brown if only to feel at one with the crowd. I felt both conspicuous and invisible, and it occurred to me that the Negro students at school might feel the same way.

Legions of celebrities joined the March including Hollywood glitterati like Charlton Heston, Marlon Brando and Burt Lancaster. Mahalia Jackson, Josephine Baker, Joan Baez and Bob Dylan performed. There were speeches by organizers and leaders. The day wore on, and we were wilting in the sun. At long last, Dr. King began to speak. He began, "I join with you today in what will go down in history as the greatest demonstration for freedom in the history of our nation," and closed by declaring, "Free at last, free at last. Thank God Almighty, we are free at last."

The March was a monumental success. It led to the passage of the Civil Rights Act of 1964 and the Voting Rights Act of 1965, which ended legally sanctioned discrimination. But more demonstrations, violence and bloodshed would follow including the bombing of the 16th Street Baptist Church in Birmingham that killed four little girls only three weeks after the March.

The movement for civil rights continued to grow in scope and reach. I was riveted to the news. The stories of struggles were conveyed in songs made popular by Sam Cooke, Pete Seeger, Phil Ochs, Mavis Staples, Odetta, Bob Dylan and Peter, Paul and Mary. I read *Black Boy* and *Native Son* by Richard Wright, and *Go Tell it on a Mountain* and *The Fire Next Time* by James Baldwin. I watched Jackie Robinson and Harry Belafonte leading protests, and listened to Nina Simone sing *Mississippi Goddam*, and Oscar Peterson play *Hymn to Freedom*.

Safe in the suburbs and white, I was insulated from the abuse and injustice that was heaped on people who were black or brown. But I felt that a revolution was at hand. I wanted to be a part of it. I started going to meetings of the local CORE (Congress of Racial Equality) group. After the bloody march in Selma in 1965, I ditched my classes to join a demonstration in front of the White House. Unlike in Selma, no one blocked or threatened me. In truth, my greatest worry was that I'd be caught on camera, and my parents would find out that I skipped school.

The Assassination

On a Friday morning in November 1963, the country was rocked by the reports that the President had been shot. I was home from school that day with a cold. Dad was with me when I heard the news. He turned on the television. Together, we watched the drama unfold. The image of the President being gunned down in broad daylight was played over and over.

I asked Dad, "What's going to happen when Johnson becomes president?"

"God only knows," he said.

It was a horrible day. All in an instant, a hero was slain. Hope was demolished. Innocence was lost.

Everything and everyone shut down for the next several days as we each absorbed the news. People my age had never lived through a world war, a Depression, a plague or a military defeat. The Dust Bowl was before our times. We had only the

Soviets to fear, and Kennedy had just backed them down in Cuba. But we were not invulnerable after all.

LBJ was sworn in late that night. Kennedy's body was flown from Dallas to the White House. It arrived, with Jackie Kennedy beside it, before dawn on Saturday morning. By the next day, thousands of mourners had gathered outside the White House in Lafayette Park.

Sunday was cold but sunny. Larry and I went downtown and waited with the throngs of mourners on Pennsylvania Avenue for the President's flag-draped coffin to roll by. Finally, we heard the sounds of drums and the clatter of horse hooves. The caisson rolled by followed by a rider-less, black horse. There was a pair of empty, backward-turned black boots strapped to the stirrups. Thousands of people stayed late into the night waiting their turn to walk by the casket in the Capitol Rotunda. On Monday, schools and government offices were closed. A million people lined the streets as the funeral procession wound from the Capitol to the White House to St. Matthew's Cathedral and on to Arlington National Cemetery. Lyndon Johnson, surrounded by the Secret Service, walked behind the caisson the entire way.

Vietnam

The threat of the Soviets loomed large throughout Kennedy's short presidency. They seemed to threaten us everywhere—in Berlin, Havana and in Vietnam. Kennedy tried to resist the pressure to send U.S. troops into South Vietnam to fight the insurgent Viet Cong. Nevertheless, the number of U.S. military in Vietnam grew from 900 to 16,000 during his brief time in office. For most, Vietnam was back-page news. We had no idea that it would soon become a dominant force in our lives.

In June, 1963, we were shocked by a searing photograph of a Buddhist monk engulfed in flames. He had set himself on fire to protest persecution by the South Vietnamese government. A year later, Congress approved the Gulf of Tonkin Resolution which gave Johnson the authority to deploy as many troops as needed to keep communists from taking over. Only two Senators dissented. It would have grave implications for us all.

Chapter 5

Michelle

I first encountered Michelle in my tenth grade typing class. I was smitten the moment I saw her. She had silken blond hair, large blue eyes, and sparkling white teeth. She was coy, sexy, and voluptuous. Baffling as it seemed, I was certain that she liked me. After all, I wasn't a great catch. I was neither a class leader nor a top student. I wasn't tall or talented or strong. I didn't own a car. When I drove one, it was my family's Rambler American station wagon, hands down the least-cool car in the world.

Typing class consisted mostly of sitting in front of an industrial-sized Smith-Corona and copying text from work books—sentences, paragraphs and formal letters. We were learning the touch system and trying not to look at our fingers. The goal was to type fast with few mistakes. A good typist could pound out 100 words per minute. I never got above 25. As the class wore on, I began to ignore the assignments and, instead, typed fanciful, semi-erotic parodies of my fellow students in the style of Terry Southern (I was reading *Candy* at the time). If the teacher came around, I'd yank out the page, crumple it, and stuff it in my notebook. Then I'd insert a fresh paper and smile at my teacher and say something like *that just wasn't up to snuff*. She would smile and walk by, thinking I was some kind of perfectionist.

Michelle sat in the next row, looking irresistible in her form-fitting mohair sweater, a pleated skirt that offered a glimpse of a thigh, and penny loafers. This was a time when people dressed modestly. Blair had a dress code. Blue jeans were outlawed. Girls were sometimes forced to kneel to show that hems of their skirts did not fall above their knees. If you dared to peg the seams of your slacks to make them thin and sleek, you had to be sure that they were loose enough to allow a ping pong ball to drop down the inside and roll out at the cuff. At any moment, the school principal might make you prove it. Needless to say, even the most modest display of femininity was apt to draw my attention, as did Michelle from the moment I saw her.

Out of boredom or curiosity, Michelle asked me to show her what I was typing. She read a bit and laughed. From then on, I tuned out the teacher and typed only to amuse Michelle. The more I wrote, the more interesting she became. I thought she was fascinating. She typed lackadaisically, paid scant attention to the teacher, and seemed to have secrets of her own. She drove a green Austin-Healey convertible with a tan leather top, and said she only went out with college guys—a rule she would soon break. Soon we were going out on actual dates and finding places to kiss and touch.

We did just about everything we could think of but screw. Contributing to our hesitancy were concerns about pregnancy which was everyone's greatest fear—just below a nuclear holocaust. We were told that abstinence was the best form of birth control. That was all well and good. But it violated every instinct known to man and boy. I personally looked forward to the day when I would shrug off the weight of my virginity. It was more than lust that drove me. It was also fear that someone would ask me if I was still a virgin. Fear of humiliation. It was only later that I fully grasped that if asked, it was easy enough to lie. Just about everyone did.

As spring turned into summer, our relationship became more intense. It felt different than the crushes and vague longings I had experienced in the past. I wanted to be around her all the time. I often went to her house in the afternoons. Once I brought Jay along. He sat down at her mother's piano and started playing tunes. I explained how he could play anything she could name—which amazed her. Then he played a couple of Johnny Mathis songs. She seemed pretty infatuated with him. After that I stopped bringing him around.

There were times that I had feelings for her that were so sharp and fitful that it felt like something was gnawing at my gut. Other times were pure bliss. Most often, my feelings ricocheted in the course of a day or even an hour from longing to despair. There were times when I wanted it to last forever. But teen love has a life of its own. It might begin with an explosion like a firecracker blasted into the air, and just as quickly crash and burn. Or it could rise in a high arc, then dissipate into the air. It's just how it happens. By the end of summer, our feelings for each other had ebbed. We stopped seeing each other every day or as often as we could. Phone calls became infrequent. We got used to gaps in conversations that had once been urgent and breathless.

On an afternoon late in August, we sat together on the couch in her living room, both knowing but not saying that this might be our last time together. In a teasing mood, she grabbed my wallet and pulled out of it the following:

    a driver's license
    three dollar bills
    a Pedro Ramos baseball card
    a Silver Spring Library card
    two ticket stubs from the Olney Theater
    a Trojan in a foil pack

"How long have you had this?" she asked, holding it up.

"A while," I said. In fact, I had bought it months earlier. For some reason, buying condoms was complicated. They were never out on the open shelves. You had to ask the pharmacist. There was always the chance that he might just say, *You're kidding. You know you're never getting laid* or something equally humiliating. But I remember steeling myself and buying a box of three Trojan-enz. I felt very cool and adult when he rang it up, took my money, put it in a plain brown bag and handed it back. Jay was waiting for me outside the drug store. When I got in the car, he looked at the box and said, "Oh shit, you got the wrong size." "What are you talking about?" "Look it says right here. These are for camels."

"I think we should test it out," I said to Michelle.

"Like an experiment?"

"More like an expression of undying love."

"Come here," she said.

Of course reality never lives up to expectations. I was nonetheless thrilled and relieved. I had finally shrugged the weighty mantel of virginity. It wasn't exactly romantic. I'm pretty sure that she did it more out of sympathy than love, which made me a little sad, but not *too* sad.

Phyllis

Later that fall, Larry and I went to the Brentano's book store to see what we might buy if we had any money to spend, which we didn't. As we walked into the store, our attention was ripped away by a vision of a girl so striking that the shop turned bright yellow and posters flew off the walls, fluttered around the store and fell softly back in their places. She wasn't a classic beauty—flawless or statuesque. But she had the kind of look about her that made me think of fresh air, sunshine and mountain streams. She was shapely and supple. Her hair was blonde and wavy. Her eyes were bright and blue, and I liked how she squinted slightly as though she was either a bit disdainful or just nearsighted. She was so lovely I forgot to breathe. My feet were leaden. Paralysis had set in.

Larry, being bolder, flew to the counter, glanced at her nametag, and, affecting his most cavalier self, asked, "Hi Phyllis. Been working here long?"

"I just started this week. Have you been here before?"

"Actually, I live here," said Larry, going off the deep edge.

"Really!" she said.

"Yeah. Upstairs in the Travel section. I sleep on a cot between Lithuania and Greece."

She gaped at him.

"So what do you do when you're not working here?" he continued. "Are you in college?"

"Hardly," she said. "I go to Blair."

I was incredulous. *How could I have not seen this girl before?*

"Perhaps you know my friend Pete? He goes to Blair."

"I'm sorry. We haven't met," she said glancing up at me prettily.

"Not only that," Larry added, "he's a famous child actor. Very big on the Borscht Circuit."

"No kidding? So what brings you guys in here?" she asked.

"Books! We're looking for books." I inserted a bit too loudly.

"To buy?" she asked.

"Possibly. Not necessarily today, of course."

"Why don't you look around a bit and let me know when you are ready to buy something."

With that we were summarily dismissed. Once outside, Larry exclaimed. "Did you see that? That girl is totally into me."

"Really? I'm pretty sure she's out of your league."

"Yeah? We'll see about that," he promised.

After this encounter, I searched for Phyllis at school. I was sure she would remember me. *Yes! I'm that incredibly worldly guy you met in the bookstore.* I saw her walk by in the hallway a few times, but I never mustered the courage to talk to her. Over the next several weeks, my thoughts of Phyllis had all but faded. But at the start of the next semester, I found myself in Mr. LeBaron's Advanced Composition and Grammar in a classroom in Building A. I had just settled into my assigned seat when seconds before the class began, Phyllis entered the room and sat down at the desk in front of me. *Yes!* I thought. *There is a god!*

I spent the next several days thinking of ways to engage her with clever banter or seduce her with a soulful glance. As none of this worked, I was reduced to passing the hour by counting the tiny golden, barely visible, hairs on the nape of her neck. Then, one day, she turned and handed me a note. I started to unfold it, but she whispered, "Give this to Neal," gesturing toward the guy behind me. I complied. Then Neal handed me his response, which gave me a reason to tap on her shoulder. She smiled ever so slightly. This got old quickly. The next time she handed me a note, I opened it up as if to read it. Phyllis watched incredulously. Then I ripped it into tiny pieces and handed them back to her.

She seemed both startled and annoyed, but from that moment on, she took an interest in me not previously demonstrated. From then on, Phyllis and I found ways to withstand the unbearable tedium of the last class of the day. We talked in whispers, commenting on the teacher's strange aspects (*drunk or not drunk?*). We named other students after literary characters. (Alvin Rothman was Admiral Hornblower because he wore jack boots.) We told each other which authors we liked the best and what books we were reading (*Catch 22, Wuthering Heights*), and we walked together to our lockers at the end of class. Being together felt easy and comfortable, and I was sure that we were meant for each other. But our timing was off. She was already going with some guy named Mike. And, by the time we became close, my attention—and lustful inclinations—had been pulled in another direction.

Sue S.

One early spring afternoon, Jay and I sat high up in the auditorium watching a succession of students performing in the school talent show. It was easy to make fun of them from up there, but I admired their nerve. Also, some of them could actually sing in tune on occasion or dance to the actual beat—neither of which I could claim to do. Then, unexpectedly, a girl I'd never noticed before stepped onto the stage. She was slender and lithe and had clear, flawless skin, dark flashing eyes and long black hair that fell to her waist. She stood in front of the mike, strummed a guitar and sang a Gordon Lightfoot song, *That's What You Get for Loving Me*. It was sad and haunting.

Don't you shed a tear for me
'Cause I ain't the love you thought I'd be
I got a hundred more like you
So don't be blue
I'll have a thousand 'fore I'm through.

I was in love by the second chorus.

"She's not a bad singer. And she's gorgeous." I pointed out.

"You got that right."

"I have to have that girl."

"Fat chance," said Jay.

Her name was Sue S. After the talent show, I frequently noticed her gliding past with the grace of a panther. She didn't seem to be with anyone in particular. But then she didn't seem particularly interested in anyone either. She just had this nice, self-assured way about her like she was thinking *I'm only here for you to see and appreciate but actually I don't need any of you at all.*

I wracked my brain thinking of ways to meet her. I didn't know anybody who knew her. Standing out from the crowd and attracting attention from strange girls was not my forte. I was pretty sure that there were some secret things you could say that would captivate girls, but I had no idea what they were.

At the time, I was working on the weekends at a stable that was an off-shoot of the summer camp that I'd been going to for years. It had all the usual camp activities—swimming, shooting guns and arrows, playing capture the flag—but mostly it was a horse camp. It had a string of horses named after states (*Tennessee, Texas,* etc.) or Santa's reindeer (*Donder, Blitzen*), but my favorite ones to ride were the lighting fast ponies (*Shadow* and *Blue*) that I could hop on bareback and tear up the hills or around the lake, not caring if I fell off or not.

At the stable, I brushed and saddled horses, mucked stalls, and taught little kids how to ride. (*Squeeze with your knees until your teeth hurt*) Camp Waredaca, the stables, the Butts family (camp owners) and everyone I worked alongside was my *other* world—my life away from school, family and friends. Working as a camp counselor was like stepping into an earlier time. We slept in cabins and crapped in outhouses. We rode horses, bucked hay, and went skinny dipping in the lake while the campers were sleeping. Camp was also my entrée into the world of *horse people* who could talk endlessly about breeds, and how many hands high a horse was and what are the best brands of boots and tack. There was no bridge between my two worlds until Sue walked in. I flipped when I saw her and blinked to be sure I wasn't dreaming. There she was, a few feet away, combing the mane of an Arabian mare that was as sleek and black and shiny as her long hair. And there I was, pitchfork in hand, pushing a wheelbarrow full of horse manure. This was my big chance. *What would Cary Grant say to Grace Kelly at a time like this? Or Rock Hudson to Doris Day?*

"I'm sorry." It was all I could muster. "I was just about to rake out this stall."

She looked down at my mud-caked boots. "You work here?" she asked.

"Nah. I like to shovel shit for the fun of it."

She laughed. "Well in that case, you can shovel my stall anytime," she said lasciviously, or so it seemed to me.

She told me that she just started boarding her horse at the stable. I asked her about her how long she had him and where she liked to ride. She asked how I got the job and whether I had a horse. We talked about how much we loved horses—their power and speed and how some of them are calm and wise and others were head cases just like a lot of people we knew.

When I saw her at school, she seemed happy to see me. We laughed about meeting in a stall. Soon we looked for each other in the halls or cafeteria or in the smoking grove behind the parking lot. I smoked Marlboros. She smoked Parliaments. We talked about horses and riding and what a drag everything was compared to flying down a rough trail, when your horse is just slightly out of your control, and feeling scared and exhilarated at the same time. A few weeks later, I asked her to go with me out to Gaithersburg to a horse auction. She said ok. A few days later we drove there together. I parked the car in the field behind the show barn. Instead of going in, we sat in the car listening to the Beatles sing *Eight Days a Week*. In the middle of it, we started kissing, and it seemed like we would never stop. After that, Sue and I were pretty much inseparable, and I was in bliss.

When senior year rolled around, everyone was obsessing about where to apply to college. Some students going on college tours with their parents, but I thought it would be more fun to go with four guys from school—including one with access to a Pontiac. We came up with a list: *Harvard, MIT, Yale, Wesleyan and Connecticut College.* I had no hope of getting into any of them. But I didn't want to pass up a road trip. My compatriots, however, were top students and actually had a shot. So off we went.

We had a great three days and went on several campus tours. I dozed off during a class at MIT. We spent two nights in dorms at Harvard and Yale. When we got back to school on Monday morning, the school counselor went crazy because we had left without telling anyone. Apparently, they like to know if you plan to disappear for three days. He said that if he had anything to do with it, none of us would go to any college. Since we were sure that our futures depended on getting into the right school, we were in a panic. But later he settled down, and nothing bad came of it.

After getting turned down by a number of rarified colleges, I was relieved to be accepted to Earlham College, where my brother, Dick, was finishing his junior year. He was a good student, so they probably felt they had to let me in. That spring, I had a bout of senioritis and I barely passed chemistry. I was happy when the semester came to an end. Yearbooks were handed out on the last day. Phyllis asked me to write in hers, and she wrote in mine:

Dear Peter. I'm sure you already know how I feel. After graduation, I'm sure I'll never see you again because where and when would that happen? Without your vibrating remarks, our talks of Franny and Zooey, and visions and revisions, along with you tearing up my note that fateful day—this year would have stunk. Damn it. I'll miss you. Love. Phyllis.

At last, we had graduated from high school. Larry from Northwood, the rest of us from Blair. Jay too, although there were still a few credits he had to earn over the summer. I went back to work at Camp Waredaca that summer for a final time. At the end of August, I would leave for Earlham. Bob was headed to the University of North Carolina, and Cooper to the University of Maryland. Larry and Levy would be attending Montgomery Junior College in Silver Spring, as would Phyllis.

The night before I left Silver Spring, we drained a bottle of *Johnny Walker Red* that Bob had purloined from his father's liquor cabinet. We talked into the night about how it was just the beginning and how each of us would be successful beyond our dreams. "Pretty soon we'll be getting together at somebody's posh apartment on Central Park West or at some mountain lodge in the Rockies like the one in *North by Northwest*," Larry said.

We agreed that Bob would become an architect who designed buildings in New York, Chicago and Singapore. Jay would be a famous recording artist. I'd write my novel. Larry would become famous as a talk show host, and Cooper would be a beat poet and underground entrepreneur. We'd all be loaded and own Corvettes or Porches or BMWs. I'd be driving a Jaguar XKE.

"Damn straight," Bob concurred.

I knew then that the center of my universe was about to shift. Going away to college would be the first step. Whatever came next would take me even farther away. I felt nervous, excited and somehow disloyal.

"I'm going to miss you guys," I said as we emptied the bottle.

"We'll miss you too," Larry said. "And for chrissakes, write us a letter once in a while."

Chapter 6

Freshman Year

It wasn't easy, but I survived the awkwardness of my parents delivering me and all my stuff (clothes, typewriter, stereo, records, Mark Cross pen set, fresh underwear, etc.) to college.

Earlham, a liberal arts college of just over 1,000 students, was founded by Quakers. It had a liberal orientation that was at odds with the surrounding community of Richmond, Indiana. There was not much in the area to recommend it. The most compelling landmark was a swimming hole in an abandoned quarry. Outside the city limits, there was nothing but farms, pastures and corn fields.

Dean Curtis welcomed the freshmen with platitudes: *Make the most of this opportunity. Become good friends. Be true to your school.* There were picnics, games, and discussion groups which offered all kinds of opportunities to scope out candidates for carnal exploration. But we did learn about the school and its traditions and rules.

> *No drinking on campus.*
> *No men in the women's dorms.*
> *Women must be in their dorms by curfew.*
> *Convocations are mandatory.*
> *Only upper classmen may live off-campus.*

What have I gotten into? I wondered. Back home, I was exploring new ways to ignore convention, defy authority and skirt the law. Here I would be a captive of *in loco parentis*, the purpose of which was to constrain, repress or extinguish all natural and compelling urges.

I was excited when classes began. In Humanities we were assigned a book *(Utopia, Last Days of Socrates, The Fable of the*

Bees, Till We Have Faces) to read and a paper to write each week. I worked late into the night, typing away on my portable Smith-Corona, to finish the papers in time—only to have them critiqued to the extent it undercut any notion I had that I knew how to write. It was a painful lesson.

I soon got into a rhythm of reading, writing, playing bridge and scouting out coeds. On Friday nights, I helped run *The Green Dolphin*, an ersatz night club in the basement of our dormitory. We couldn't serve booze, but we were able to bring in a band or play taped dance music (*Hang on Sloopy, Louie Louie, Satisfaction*). There was a student-run coffee shop called the *Guarded Well By* that hosted budding folk singers and poets. Usually there was a movie showing in Carpenter Hall. Truffaut, Fellini and Hitchcock were favored directors. We were nothing if not pretentious.

I was enjoying campus life and getting to know people, but I missed my friends and wondered what I was missing. After a few weeks, we began to correspond. Larry's letters were delirious and hyperbolic. Jay's were pure stream of consciousness.

September 25, 1965 (From PB to LH and JL)

Dear Larry and Jay,

I should have written earlier but was waiting more for the right frame of mind than anything else. I don't know quite where to start except to say that I'm enjoying the hell out of it.

The campus is replete with ivy-covered buildings surrounding a grassy area called the Heart. There are six dormitories, and many more classroom buildings, labs, and assembly halls (the first dating back to the 1800s) and a new, Japanese style library which is airy and clean. It also has a gym, a Quaker meeting house, and a stable. The campus is right off I-70, and rumor has it that every year a motorcade of Ku Klux Klan members in white hoods drive past the campus. Apparently, Indiana is the birthplace of the Klan.

My roommate is a physics major from Cincinnati. It is odd to be living in a space that's the size of a coffin with someone I don't have a thing in common. But he's pretty quiet which is just as well. I'd hate to be stuck in a room with someone who bores you to death. Most of the guys are cool. There's a guy from Texas whose folks have a ranch of about 100,000 acres. He speaks with a drawl. Of course we call him Tex. He plays the guitar, rides and ropes, and has an uncanny ability to walk up the walls by wedging his feet on one side of the hallway with his hands on the other, and inching his way up from the floor to ceiling. I'm not sure exactly what this is good for but it's cool to watch.

Another freshman, John May, and I are running this little night spot in the basement called the Green Dolphin. It's a place to go for music and dancing when there's nothing else happening. I like John, but he has the terrible habit of being very cheerful and friendly the moment he wakes up in the morning that makes me want to kill him.

It's weird to live in a place where there are so many young women in such close proximity. As soon as we got here, they handed out this thing called the Wolf Book which has pictures of all the freshmen. Everyone immediately rifled through it trying to identify the babes and figure out how to lay claim before anyone else does. It's like everyone is in a hurry panning for gold in the same small stream.

The pickings are slim. It's definitely not like walking down the boardwalk at Ocean City where every girl is a knock-out. I guess everyone is way too scholarly or something. Nevertheless, there are a few who I'm slightly interested in getting to know. The thing is that none of them compare to Sue S., which makes me crazy because I'm trying not to think about her at all but its goddam hard not to.

I'm pretty jazzed about my classes, my tall pile of expensive text books. I'm enjoying all the various dormitory shenanigans and breathing in all this fresh Hoosier air.

I already miss you guys. I keep thinking that sometime I will see an elephantine white Chrysler coming down the street -- that you and Levy will hop out of the car, and we'll smoke a couple of cigarettes together. The thought makes me both happy and sad.

Write soon. I long to hear about your escapades and what you are thinking, reading, the music you are listening to and about anyone you are screwing—or more accurately—who you would like to be screwing.
Write soon and send me Ochsman's address.
Pete

A response came in just a few days.

September 29, 1965 (From LH to PB)

Mon Ami,

I sigh heavily, laugh, yell and whoop a few times, bend my head and shed a few small tears of happiness at hearing your long absent voice. I jump up and down three times in quick succession, grab a sheaf of paper and typewriters, and light a cigarette (a Camel if you must know). I rush to the record player and slap on five Brubeck records and begin.

God. Jesus. What can I tell you of life on my beautiful, ivy-less campus? Nothing? No, there is a lot to tell. First off, I like it. I mean I really do like it, and it saddens me to hear the student body complain about what a terrible place it is. It's small, uninspiring, and spiritless but not terrible for crying out loud.

I dropped Zoology so I now take 14 credits and I cope with them fairly well. French offers me trauma but I plan to manage it somehow. I switched English teachers after a full day of begging, lying, crying, praying and running around having forms signed. The new teacher, Mr. Henry, has a face exactly like a Boston Bull Terrier. He is cynical, bitter and terrifically exciting. Levy loves him and sits behind me quietly laughing through an entire lecture while I jump up and down guffawing and embarrassing our young piano player.

My other classes are standard, no complaint and no academic thrill, either. But in Sociology I find heaven in a long-haired girl, thin and lithe who does not know I exist. My heart breaks as I compose poem after poem that she will never see. 'Tis sad, omigod, so sad.

The weird thing, almost scary, is that besides Levy and Watkins and a few persons of little note that attended either Blair or Northwood, I haven't met anybody new or different. (It is sad because one must broaden one's horizons at college, or so I am told.)

I saw Sue S. the other day as I sped past our alma mater going at least 85 mph. She looked lovely in the autumn sunshine but as she called my name (somewhat hysterically), I steeled myself and pressed my size eleven loafer even harder on the accelerator. You are now permitted, due to this act of unexcelled self-control, to address all further correspondence to "Faithful Friend."

I would like to send you Bob's address but no one has heard from the genius and at last notice they were sending a group of state troopers into the Carolina hills armed with slide rules in order to lure him back to his responsibilities.

Susie and I see each other often and seem to enjoy it, miracle of miracles, I think I like her more and more every time we are together. Last Friday night we had a very interesting tete a tete at her house complete with a steak dinner, wine, violent frustrating love making, declarations of affection, the whole sticky mess—but I like it.

Levy and Lorraine maintain the eternal status quo which is nice, I suppose. She is struggling through Maryland U. but will probably make it, like all of us.

Larry

Since the Earlham campus was dry and rule-bound, most of the anticipated college antics were taking place in the houses where upper classmen lived. While freshmen and sophomores had to live on campus, older male students were permitted to find their own accommodations, while women were allowed only to live in dorms or in college-owned off-campus houses where the prohibitions against drinking and fornication still prevailed.

There were other diversions as well. I signed up to write for the *Earlham Post*. There were football and soccer games (our teams were called the *Fighting Quakers*), intramural sports, socials and dances, and theatrical or music performances by students and touring professionals, including the Julliard String Quartet. There were political forums and discussions. Vietnam was the most frequent topic. And every day, a dozen or so students stood in a silent vigil during the lunch hour to protest the war.

I wasn't sure what to make of it. My father had enlisted in the Army during World War II but was classified 4-F because of his lousy eyesight. He went to Turkey as part of the Office of Information Services. I don't know if he was ever in danger. I do know that he came home with a yen for yogurt, curry and other exotic fare.

One forum discussed alternatives to enlistment and whether it was possible to abide by the law and your conscience at the same time. It seemed a bit theoretical, since we all had student deferments that would likely be continued as long as we were in college or graduate school. The question of military service didn't seem urgent. But it was top of mind for anyone close to graduating.

General Hershey, the head of the Selective Service, spoke at an all-campus convocation. He was giving a speech about duty to country, but these were not the times for platitudes. Students pressed him on the morality of fighting an unjust war. The more he defended American intervention, the more the hisses and jeers. There was a stark contrast between the imperious General and the scruffy students, who were getting increasingly rude. It got to be uncomfortable, particularly for the school administrators and Quaker professors who valued peaceful attempts to build consensus. Finally, Hershey stalked off the stage.

Ironically, it was Hershey who helped establish alternatives to military service for conscientious objectors during World War II. But no one seemed aware of it at the time.

There have always been war resisters. During World War I, the Selective Service Act recognized objectors from certain religious sects. Instead of being forced into combat, they were put to work in army camps where they were often abused by enlisted soldiers. Others went to prison. Before World War II, the Mennonites and Quakers lobbied to have conscientious objectors assigned to civilian duties or noncombatant service in the military. In response, Hershey set up Civilian Public Service which allowed C.O.'s to work for the forest service, on farms or be guinea pigs in scientific tests. There were 50,000 registered objectors during World War II, and 170,000 during the war in Vietnam. Some 300,000 more applied but were turned down. You could only be a conscientious objector if you could prove that you believed in God. An agnostic or atheist had no legal claim, until the Supreme Court ruled differently in 1965. But even then, draft boards did what they wanted to do. All told, more than half a million men illegally evaded the draft. A third were charged with an offense. More than 50,000 fled to Canada or other countries or went underground.

As the weeks wore on, Vietnam drove much of what was talked about. Under General Westmoreland, the number of American troops escalated, and the body count climbed. U.S. and South Vietnamese forces stopped at nothing in their effort to eradicate the Viet Cong. As one officer declared: *We had to destroy the village in order to save it.*

October 21, 1965 (from LH to PB)

Pete,

By now I suppose you have heard in broad terms from Levy of my recent move. I sure as hell needed you around to talk to. Anyway I've sent in my application to the Peace Corps for a really fantastic variety of reasons. I think that you, more than anyone else deserve to know them.

First of all is my swiftly deteriorating family life. It gets worse and worse and I have no place to run to. Secondly, but even more pressing, is the fact that I find, after six weeks of college, that I'm accomplishing nothing. I can't get over this terrific disappointment. MJC is not thrilling, it is stifling. Like my English teacher said today, "You're kidding yourself if you think MJC is a college. It's not."

Thirdly, I suddenly feel the desire to do something that takes a minimum of waiting. But it seems as though before I'm allowed to do anything I have to pay my dues. According to good old society, we must do certain things in a certain prescribed order. I'm sick and tired of doing what is expected rather than what I want. It boils down to this. I take the test on November 11th and if things go right I'll finish the school year and take off.

Jay and I both thought your article in the Post was well written and hope to see more of your journalistic pearls. The Green Dolphin sounds cool and probably will be the scene of Ramsey Lewis's next recording session. Jay was touched by your concern for his post-accident mental condition. For a while he was in a bad way but lately he's been fine. Lorraine is out of the hospital and the car soon will be fixed.

Life in its cruddy way goes on. Try and bring that Tex guy home with you for Christmas so I can learn how to walk up the walls. I tried to do it in Levy's apartment l and fell on my ass.
Let me hear from you more often.
Larry
P.S. I read Hapworth 16 a week or two after you left and was delighted, puzzled and amazed. Now I'm starting Herzog. It is out in paperback and is really terrific.

It was good to hear that he was thinking about joining the Peace Corps. It seemed like a good thing to venture from the comforts of home. Of course, the Peace Corps might take him oceans away.

October 27, 1965 (letter from PB to LH)
Larry,

I share this room with a guy from Cincinnati. At one end there is a heater that extends the width of the room. There is a very broad and tall window which I like to leave open as wide as possible. Sometimes it gets quite cold. The heads of the two beds are against the wall, and there is a desk between the beds. At the end of my bed is my desk on which I'm typing now. Over it is a bulletin board that I found in the basement. Next to the bulletin board is a bookcase. In the bookcase there about 15 books which I brought from home and another 10 paperbacks I bought for my courses. There is also a bottle of Crisco oil, a popcorn popper, a bag of popcorn, a bottle of Mennen's aftershave and two unwashed coffee mugs.

There is a small maple tree outside the window. Most of its leaves have fallen. Beyond that there is a service building and a parking lot, and the gym. That's as far as I can see. I can't see you or Levy or the field in which we drink Jack Daniels but I have this terribly real feeling that I know what you are thinking about three seconds before you think it yourself. (I dig what you're thinking.)

Now here's what I'm thinking. Do it Larry, for chrissakes, if it is at all possible, do it man. It may surprise you, I don't know - it surprises me a little - but I feel strongly that you should go through with it if it means that much to you. Let me leave it at that. It is heartfelt.

All right. I've got letters to write to home and my sister and my grandfather, Lorraine, and Sue S. (I've yet to write her) and four other people and to you.

One other comment (in half-assed and hysterical seriousness.) Write to me Lar. Your letter is horribly incomplete. Where are your prolonged, insufferable exaggerated, bull-shitting, embellished, untrue and beautiful stories of people and things and places that I refuse to take without a grain of salt?
Pete Berliner

No sooner had I written, than I got what I was hoping for— one of Larry's patented tales of adventure and woe.

October 30, 1965 (letter from LH to PB)
Dear Pete,

It is growing colder now and becoming runny nose weather for all of us. The leaves are mostly fallen and the streets grow thick with big dead piles of them, red brown and gold and yellow. It is October, and like herring coming home to spawn, Laurie and I are drawn to each other. I think of her, still loving her in a sort of remote and objective way. After thousands of arguments with myself I go to her, and we talk and nothing more—but that's okay with me.

She tells me of her life, her drunken happiness, her sensual adventures, and her love for me and for life. I listen and drive my little car deeper into the country near the Butts farm, in an attempt to rid myself of the choking feeling that I feel most of the time. Finally I have a chance to talk. I tell her of my life, the Peace Corps, your letters and my loves.

I will talk to anyone non-stop. I want terribly for everyone to understand, to dig, to attain some insight into my life, and I want to have some understanding of theirs. It rarely works out that way. With Laurie and me, we dig and feel an inner something about each other but of course the natural "Let's go lie down somewhere, baby," remains unsaid.

Sex, its mystery and magic was, I hasten to tell you, revealed to me in a dizzying night several weeks ago on my parents' warm bed.

Alexis, fresh out of a convent where she gave birth to a seven pound baby boy, called and asked me to get together one night.

"We used to have such nice discussions," she says.

"Yeah, sure." I answer. "What do you like to drink?"

So the following Saturday I steal a decanter of Wolfschmidtz Vodka from my dad's well stocked cabinet and pick her up. It's cold outside. She's wearing dark stockings and an empire waist thing that is so short it leaves nothing but the essentials unshown. I maintain a cool which reminds one of an ancient Stoic. After some banal nonsense she asks, "Where are we going?"

"I don't know, I thought we could drop in on Levy's apartment but his girl is in the hospital."

"Oh."

"Don't worry my parents are out and I suppose I can make use of my house. My brothers won't bother us too much."

"Okay." I shift gears and pull into Drug Fair parking lot. "I have to get something here," I say simply meaning tomato juice for the drinks. "Come on in with me."

"No," she says, "you go in there and get whatever you get (meaning rubbers) and need. I'll wait in the car."

For three strained minutes I argue with her to come into the store with me until I realize that she thinks I'm going in for rubbers. Then I laugh and we take off.

At my house, I mix drinks and put on some Ahmad Jamal, and she tells me of the agonies of birth. We discuss our philosophies of sex. I quote Hemingway. She smiles cryptically. I await the inevitable. I get high. Sliding almost into her goddam lap, I place my gentle hand on her tiny breasts and whisper: "Can I make sweet love to you?" "Yes, "she says, and lunges on top of me.

I suggested that we retire to the boudoir and we do. Fast, everything happens too fast but I stay cool. Her clothes fall in a pile in the corner. I smile and think that I'm in charge of the situation. She unbuckles my pants and grabs my sex and I have doubts as to who is in charge. It turns out she is on the rag. "JESUSCHRISTALMIGHTY," I think to myself.

"Do you want me?" she says.

What to say. What to say.

I say, "Not now, let's wait for a better time."

She groans and says, "No it's safe now. Just a little messy."

What the shit is going on here, I think. Is this any way to ruin a bed?

She goes to the toilet to prepare herself, and I slip on one of the old man's Trojans. We start again. I remember her hair, long and black, in my face and her long white legs wrapped, almost tangled, with mine, her skin pale and soft. It was oh so swell.

So much for the sordid aspect of my insignificant life.

Levy and I have a place where truth, hard to find, occasionally is born. High atop the administration building is a room where Music Appreciation is taught. It is rarely filled and an ancient tumbledown piano lives there. I heard it being played one day during the first week of school and mentally filed it away so if ever Levy should say, "Christ I feel like playing", I could take him there. Now if we're together for a free hour or two, and walking sadly through the fallen leaves and not talking and he says to me "Let's go play the piano," we smile and hurry up the marble steps and close the door. Then he takes off his cashmere jacket and switches his sunglasses for his regular glasses (a ritual I see him repeat at least a thousand times a day). He sits nervously down while I light an illegal cigarette and pray for greatness.

Above the piano, on the wall, is a chart made out of sections of pegboard and plastic letters with all the various musical periods and the great composers and dates of that period. One day I will sit down and read that chart for the 800th time while Levy plays Nomad, and down at the bottom, as if it's been there for a millennia, in the modern section, right after Gershwin, it will say Jay Levy. The funny thing is that this is exactly the kind of stuff I can't speak to Levy about. He just doesn't understand. We tell each other everything, but the truth is he can never know himself I as well as I know him, and he can never love me as I love him. His heart, and it makes me cry at times, is not as big as it should be.

And, I also fear that he will never be happy because he tends to overlook the tiny things (unless he is drunk) that bring joy to my overly sentimental heart. As you know, the strange thing is that you are 600 miles away and hold most of the answers. Sweet shit. Life.

Questions, questions, questions, questions: Am I really younger and less mature than I should be because I refuse to accept the patterns of accepted conduct? (Cruddy sentence). Am I a jerk because the colors of autumn thrill the hell out of me, or because I'm very sad/happy at the very sight of my little brother playing football and because I don't really want to grow up?

Look Pete. Tell your private God to make Christmas vacation come very quickly. I have a terrible desire to stuff this envelope with two cigarette butts I smoked while I was typing, an empty can of Right Guard, a batch of love poems that Susie sent me, a little drawing I did on my sociology notes, a bottle of ink, my lighter, some loose pages of a novel my brother threw at me, an old issue of Time magazine, the shift knob from my VW, some Halloween candy, movie ticket stubs from The Knack, the wax from my ears, some cuttings from recent haircut, etc. etc. etc. In a brief sentence, hurry home. I've got a lot of things to tell and discuss and you need to see my hysterical face in order to get their full meaning.

Your girl (?) Sue S. called a few days ago. She is sad and angry with you because you don't write. She misses you and wants you and (in her words) is lost and confused and mixed up without you. She said she never realized how deep her feelings were for you until you were gone. I think that is very nice to have some girl yearn for you in that way, so maybe you should write her. I told her that you were screwing every night and were probably drunk most of the day.

I got a letter from Ox. The school sounds very much like the Chicago Playboy Club without the bunnies. He is sad without girls and describes his situation as "shitty". There are 11 boys to every girl on campus. But the entertainment is amazing. So far he has seen two Brubeck concerts at the college and will soon be seeing Nancy Wilson and Louis Armstrong. The drinking is amazing. There is a guy who runs a private bar out of his dorm room which they refer to as Whiskey a Go Go. Bob sounds happy but horny. He is maintaining a 3.0 average. Levy says he could have not told us about his goddamn average very easily buddy, very easily.

Bob's address is 734 Morrison Resident College, F house, University of North Carolina at Chapel Hill, North Carolina.

I sit here as my parents leave for dinner out. A freshly lit cigarette is in my mouth. My brothers and their peers are screaming outside because they have just seen a real ghost. The doorbell is ringing and I don't want to stop this letter simply to give out bags of M&Ms to little kids in disguise.

Levy and Lorraine and Dave Levin and his date will soon see Oscar Brown at the Cellar Door. Susie S. is in New Jersey for the weekend, and Alexis can't come over. My car has little or no gas in it. I am penniless. I've just eaten two chicken pot pies, and I think I'm going to barf. My eyes smart from three hours of studying this afternoon in Maryland's cavernous library, and you are damn far away.

Write soon and make it epic.

Larry

I got a letter from Jay on the same day.

October 30, 1965 (letter from JL to PB)

Somewhere in the Western World

Peterberliner

Received your letter and my only comment is on JD Salinger and his pig pen Zen is "Bosh!" I suppose ever since I read Teddy in Nine Stories and keep catching Larry snatch glances from The Catcher in the Rye, I have decided that Salinger is ruining anybody who believes most of his hogwash. No offense, I hope.

Getting back to the vagina of things, I really must say I enjoyed your letter, and most certainly your article in the Earlham Post. Your letter came at a time when I really needed to hear from someone whom I haven't seen every day. I thought your "In Crowd" article was rather terrific; Larry was the most jealous bastard I've ever seen when he saw how terrifically the thing was organized, and what a damn nifty and cute little vocabulary you have. We both agreed because you don't say things over and over like I do—like really, terrific and you know. The only thing I was wondering was about this. I wonder how much Ramsey Lewis could make by cutting singles of the Green Dolphin Street, Satin Doll, or any other songs contained in the album but are superior musical compositions to "In Crowd." I'm sure that the teen age bracket would not stop twice to listen to any of these compositions because they involve too many harmonic complexities, which would either confuse their 1-4-5 chord minds or simply bring curseful reactions.

Since we're on the topic of sounds I might add that I'm progressing in my piano playing at a rate of learning something in three months it would take someone two weeks to learn if taught by a qualified professional. But that's how it goes. School hasn't been too bad and every once in a while a few instructors get together, hold me down by the arms and legs, and force some knowledge down my ungrateful throat, hoping that it will somehow reach my brain. Lorraine was forced to miss this semester because of the accident (This being the main thing which made me contemplate jumping off the Calvert Street Bridge) and will return in February to either Maryland or MJC.

I suppose it has been pretty boring around here except for that sonofabitchnmotherfuckerbastardshit who ran through a red light smashing into us, hurting the person I love more than anyone in the whole damn world. I really can't tell you how it feels sitting in a horribly wrecked car, knowing that you have not been hurt, looking at a beautiful girl who was laughing and talking just two minutes ago, and is now crying with a bloody mouth and terribly afraid. I know this may sound corny but Pete, this was, without a damn doubt, the worst time of my life. But she will be alright, and she really looks better than ever. She is taking the entire ordeal so beautifully and believe it or not with humor. It makes me feel like a child to know that I sat around and cried about the whole thing for a couple of days. Well enough of this stuff.

You mentioned that you would try to write her. If you haven't already, I really wish you would. She misses you like crazy, just like I do, and a letter just to her alone would make her feel better. I know you are busy, but please try.

Oh yeah, Larry is joining the Peace Corps (no shit). He has turned in his application and is waiting to take the test on November 16th or so. He has put down that he will be available after July, 1966. This means, of course, that Horwitz is not going back to school until 1968 or 69. This has Mr. and Mrs. H. in quite an uproar. He is really serious about going (if they take him, and you can never tell). He has flatly turned down my suggestion about waiting until he completes two years at MJC. But I have a feeling he's ripping off a letter explaining what is happening and how he feels.

I did receive a letter from B.O. Plenty Ochsman and he appears to be well adjusted and full of zeal about good old campus life down south. I guess I'm just jealous of both you and Bob. But that's what I get for not doing my homework in high school. Incidentally, you seem to have a pretty sharp dorm, and I would really like to play a few sets at the Green Dolphin for a few weeks. I wish I could just jump into that crazy old Chrysler, buy some Jack Daniels, cheese (cheddar of course) and crackers and take off at about 4 o'clock in the morning and come to see your berlinerfreckled face and shoot the bull with you. I guess I'll just have to wait until you get back and we will take a trip, with Horwitz of course, somewhere, and I hope it will be like old times.

> Where are the friends that I knew in my Maying
> In the days of my youth, in the first of my roaming?

Stop screaming. I know it's corny but that sort of crap is always true and I hope it doesn't happen to us even if you win the Nobel Prize for Literature and I become an auto mechanic.

I still don't know what I'm doing or where I'm going as of yet. It gets pretty frustrating when everyone around me knows what the hell they're going to make of their life.

I wish I could tell you some funny crap or something but since you and Larry are the only guys I can talk to I'll have to tell you exactly what I feel and not a lot of funny chit chat crap. Hope I didn't bore you. Well things are not so bad lately. It helps considerably when I hear from you and B.O.

Hey, I did think of one funny thing that happened to Lar and me. We were down at the Zebra Room on Wisconsin Avenue a couple of weeks ago on a Friday night. We were sitting around getting drunk on pitchers of beers and eating Slim Jims. The place was absolutely mobbed with college kids and was so smoky that you had to stick your head into your shirt pocket in order to get some fresh air. Well we just sat around getting more crocked by the minute and not giving a damn about anything. Then some people got up and out of a booth next to us and I happened to notice a little black box on the wall on the inside of the booth. I sort of said to Larry, "Hey what in the god damn hell is that little old black box on the wall right there"

And he said, "That's one of them bastard fuse boxes for Christ's sakes."

I said, "I'll guess I'll have to look inside that cunt right now."

He said, "Yeah why not."

So I start to look inside and sure enough there about 20 different glass fuses. Well, I started turning them off but nothing I could see was happening. Finally I got the right ones and began turning the lights on and *off in the restaurant so it was making little flashes. I didn't give a damn, I was really pretty drunk. Larry just kept sitting there, and a lot of people in there were laughing, and we were having a damn good time. Then this big-ass guy comes flying out of the kitchen door and I beat it back to the table, looking as innocent as a virgin.*

He walks up to old Larry and me, grabs our beer off the table, punches me in the arm, and screams at us about how I have been turning off the lights in the kitchen, and all the employees have been running around bumping into pots and pans and each other. And in true Western tradition, he throws us out the front door onto the sidewalk.

He stood there in the doorway, and yelled "Don't ever let me catch you bastards in this place again." But we didn't care as we were drunk as hell.

Well, I guess that's about it for now. Please write to me whenever you get a chance because I really enjoy your letters like crazy. And by the way, say hello to the guy in your dorm who walks on the ceiling, he sounds kind of wild. I've been trying to do what he does but so far I've only succeeded in getting hair stains and footprints on the wall.

Your Scheisskopf Friend,

JML

Enc. Four barrels of Cassite Motor Honey.

I missed that sort of madness. Life at Earlham seemed much too serious and staid. I was inundated with assignments and grounded by not having a car. Opportunities for adventure and mayhem were limited. But it wasn't all bad. I was swept up in the classes, the books we read, the questions we raised. I thrilled at writing papers that started out with probing questions like *Should a law—just or unjust—ever be disobeyed? As Socrates asks in the Crito, "In leaving Athens, do I not desert the principles which were acknowledged by us to be just?"* and turn them in after hours of laborious typing, correcting errors with typewriter erasers that smeared ink across the page or white-out that gummed up the typewriter ribbon so that anything I typed after that was a flaming mess. But I digress. Larry just forwarded his latest epistle.

November 14, 1965 (letter from LH to PB)

Having just read the Magna Carta and a chapter in sociology entitled "Deviations from the Norm" and watched a show on CBS about the rotten stinking god-damn war in Vietnam, I am suddenly taken with a terrific desire to speak with you about several problems, hopes, dreams, fears, jokes and intricate little tales (served with ample bullshit) that have been filling up my simple little head for many long and dizzying days.

I dialed your number but (alas) your mother told me with a homey little chuckle that you are not expected until the 11th of December--a date which, I might add, seems very far off indeed.

So now I am warmly sitting in my bed (the one farthest from the window) with my Indian woolen blanket around my long legs, my typing necessities falling into the valley-like folds of my bedding, a Winston burning between my somewhat chapped lips, and the smoke hurting my eyes which are hidden behind my glasses with the new frames, and writing you this rather confused and perhaps incoherent letter which you will read and hopefully think about for an hour or a minute.

I am immediately struck with the overall responsibility of telling you, unbeknownst to the lady herself, how fully happy and bloated with joy Lorraine was with your latest release which to my ear sounded like a true pouring forth from the heart. Of course, she now awaits your arrival with (literal) open arms.

Are you lonely Pete? My God how unhappy and blue your letters sometimes sound to me. Not the whole thing - not at all - but certain well-modulated sentences and even occasional paragraph makes me wonder about your happiness. Is it that you feel a little lost or simply that you are not up to the push-pull responses that sometimes are so necessary for anything to develop? Why is it so hard for people, everyone, to open their secret hearts to everyone else?

I think we are all so afraid of being rebuffed that we won't take the chance. And it's sad because I know there are millions of sad and happy and wonderful things that people are carrying around with them to this day, and they are just too cautious to spill out all the goodies when anyone is near.

So in an effort to combat this strange "keeping secrets" I will tell you some nifty ones fresh in my mind and will maybe make you giggle, snort, or say shhheee.

Tale number one--with the aforementioned Alexis otherwise known as the Stealer of the Cherry or more simply—the Bedroom Tutor. Not seeing any harm in maintaining this lovely relationship I had begun with this young woman, I continue to allow her generous freedom in exploring the wonders of my genital organs (after she had expressed a desire to discontinue any further screwing).

So one night about three weeks after the amazing session in my mother's huge bed, she calls me (it was a Monday), and whispers sexily, "Can you come over?"

Seeing the chance to fend off horniness for an entire week, I answered in affirmative and rushed over, after dousing an ample amount of English Leather behind my ears.

To my surprise, she popped out of her door and said, "Let's go for a ride."

"Sure," I replied, somewhat puzzled but game.

As I drove into the lights on Georgia Avenue, I wondered what secret carnal pleasures were in store for me tonight.

Slowly, very slowly and so casually as to catch me completely off guard, she begins speaking:

"Larry"

"Huh."

"I didn't get my period yet. It's been a month and I'm a little worried."

"OHHH."

"What do you think I should do?"

"Gagghh"

"Larry?"

"Huh?"

"There's this place, Group Health. I want you to take me for a test tomorrow night so we'll know for sure. Okay?"

For a long while I was dumbfounded and articulate and completely unaware of what I should do or say. Clearly she couldn't be pregnant for several good reasons, all of which she neatly countered.

"First of all I used a rubber."

"Don't you remember, I took it off?"

"Secondly, you were on the rag."

"Sometimes that doesn't matter."

"Thirdly, it's way too early to tell. You're probably just a little late."

"I'm always regular."

The next day I became hysterical and sought advice on all fronts. First I spoke with Laurie who cried about how I could be so damn stupid and let this little bitch walk all over me. She told me to call her and tell her to forget the whole deal. If you take her for that test, "she said through her tears, "you'll be admitting you're the father of her bastard." I related the whole take to Watkins. "You better go easy," he warmed, "Cuz if she yells rape you'll be in bad trouble. Remember she's underage and you're eighteen."

Now I was at wit's end, my head was throbbing, my eyes bulging and my mind spinning with doubt and fear.

There was only one person left to see—Levy. I couldn't find him all day. Finally I went to his apartment to find him tired and grumpy after spending the last eight hours in court for the trial for his car accident. He lay on his bed listening to the new Miles Davis record with his eyes closed, and a cigarette dangling loosely from his long fingers.

"Prick," he said tiredly when I completed my tale. "You call that little bitch right now and you tell her to get fucked." His advice was so pure and uncomplicated that I followed it with only slight revisions.

I have other things to tell you about, but I want to wait until you are home so we can blow smoke and beery breath onto each other as we laugh at our own follies.

I wonder if you have heard how close Jay and I came to being there in scenic old Richmond. We planned and plotted and schemed. I spoke with your parents, and they spoke with Dick. It was to be a terrific surprise, and we were to eat Thanksgiving dinner with you. Christ were we excited. We fully planned to sneak into your room at some ungodly hour and gently begin patting you on the head ala Mr. Antonelli. It would have been nice to have spent those few days together but like a lot of things you want real bad, it just didn't work out. Sorry.

I wish I could empty myself of a lot of things that are swimming around in my brain but it's not easy to do it just like that for chrissakes. I *just like to think that sometimes you're doing something—riding a bike, taking a walk, reading a book, looking out the window, kissing a girl, saying a prayer, drinking a coke, looking at the stars, farting or whatever and you suddenly feel the emptiness I feel knowing that whenever I'm doing something—smoking a butt, shifting into third, watching my face in the mirror, or speaking with Levy (or having him speak to me in his Magic way on the piano) —you're not here to share it with me. And corny as it may sound, it is sort of an emptiness. Because it is a long hard search until you find a kindred spirit that you want to share with, and the loss of this sought after spirit leaves a large hole in your heart.*

I know I sound a little nuts and re-reading this last paragraph I find it was written in Aramaic or Persian or something. However, ponder it for a while and dash off some encouraging words as soon as you possibly can.
Confused, but happy,
Larry

As for me, aside from a couple of tentative encounters, I wasn't involved with anyone. As others around me were already forming serious relationships, I was feeling sadly unentangled. Was I being gun-shy or too choosy?

The hard part was that I had always imagined that college would be one frat party after another. Wild orgies. Drunken brawls, lustful co-eds. It probably was like that on some campuses. Just not at a place like Earlham, where women tended to demand a modicum of respect. What was the world coming to? Betty Friedan had published *The Feminine Mystique* two years before, and new ideas and attitudes about the sexes and sex were in play. Earlham didn't even have fraternities or sororities. In the meantime, there was a sighting of Bob Ochsman, who had just come home for the weekend from UNC which apparently had the kind of parties I always imagined.

November 30, 1965 (letter from LH to PB)

Oh great and magic writer of poems. O simple minded of J.D. Salinger. Oh absent member of the wondrous team of Levyochsmanhortwitzandberliner (formerly lover of the borscht circuit). I have received your handy work and I'm glad to see the college is stimulating your mind to unexcelled heights.

However there is news to report. Oxman and his ponderous brain came into town this weekend for his brother's wedding. Levy and I, at all times models of hospitality, proceeded to create hours of fun and joy for our returning prodigal.

Friday night (by rather dubious and illegal means) we acquired a bottle of rare, costly Bourbon and retired to Levy's house where we officially began another meeting of the weekend truth forum. God how the truth did fly. One minute we spoke of chairs and tables and the next of things eternal. We ran the whole gamut of emotions—now crying, now laughing, and now peeing hysterically into the bathroom bowl.

Enlightenment sparkled on our brows and deep secret plans were made. In exactly 20 years, no matter where we are and what we are all are doing, all four of us are to meet in the men's room of Union Station and hold a reunion. What fun that will be.

My gaze now wanders to an oddly shaped cork sitting on my dresser. I'm reminded of the activities of Saturday night. Since Bob had to attend a stag for his brother, Jay and I decided to double date. Double we did: two boys, two girls, two beds and two bottles of what has to be the greatest invention since indoor plumbing. What you ask? CHAMPAGNE! Chilled to perfection and sipped with grand amounts of progressively diminishing savoir faire.

Sparkling to one's brain, it is the juice of Christ. Needless to say we have shunned Mabel (of Black Label fame) in favor of the Christian Brothers and Paul Masson. Wonder of wonders—besides all its other advantages—one suffers from no hangover after an evening of imbibing. We already have put in an order at the dispensary for an entire case of their finest stuff for a wild and carefree Christmas and New Year's holiday that we will all spend together.

And of course, despite everything I know deep in my soul, you share the main topic of Bob, Jay and my realization that all that is wrong is simply because the four of us were a team, a unit, a group, and a puzzle and now parts of this wonderful puzzle are scattered all over the place in North Carolina, in Indiana and in the suburbs of the nation's capital.

Ox, never one for deep emotional and revealing outbursts, confided that he felt a loss and an emptiness when he was away at school. Naturally we agreed but the strange and spooky thing was that even while the three of us were enjoying each other's company, we knew that the damn thing was still incomplete.

You know that in times of stress (which occur fairly often these days), Levy will turn to me and I to him and say excitedly, "Let's go see Pete." But somehow or another we never are both hysterical at the same time, and the one who happens to be rational points to the bald and exhausted tires on my noble VW.

It's sad and at the same time beautiful that we miss you like this. It's too damn bad that we will have to wait until Jesus' birthday til we see you and trade with you our secret loves and personal sadnesses and happinesses.

Attention! I think you should be getting some correspondence from the Peace Corps soon (unless it's waiting for you at home). They have your college address so watch the mail. I took the test on Saturday, walking into the civil service examination room slightly hungover but full of zip. The test was mostly language aptitude with an entire hour in French.

All the people on my list of references have received their forms, and my mother has been getting hysterical calls from Lorraine, your mother, and assorted others wanting to know what to do. My mother just smiles patiently and answers even though she's against the whole thing.

The clock is ticking, Alexis is waiting for my caresses. I must conclude. But before I get the hell off the page, let me beg and plead with you to please write more often and please make your letters more complete and worthy of your wealth and talents. You see the thing is that sometimes I'm not sure if you're still there.
Larry

After the end of the term, I boarded an all-night bus back home. We had gotten little rest over the past week as we crammed for exams, and were desperate to sleep. One of the other students actually stretched out in the overhead luggage rack. After arriving home, I divided my time between family gatherings and catching up with friends.

I was always short on cash, so I got a job at the Post Office jumping from a truck delivering packages to porches and door steps, as often as not dodging dogs that had been left unchained in front of their homes. The small, yappy ones were the worst. I worked for about a week. It was cold and miserable, and I didn't get off work until well after dark.

After work one night, I finally made it over to see Sue S. She looked dazzling, as she always had. She greeted me with a hug and a kiss.

"Where have you been?"

"College, of course."

"No, I mean since you got home. I've been waiting for you to come over."

"You know. Parents. Work. All that stuff. I feel like I'm being bounced around like a tennis ball."

"I've missed you," she said. Then there was a long pause. *(Say something, jackass!)*

"Yeah. Me too. I've thought about you a lot."

"I can't stand it," she said. "We need to be together."

"Yeah. That would be great," I said, but without a lot of enthusiasm.

We went out that night and a couple times more before I went back to school. God she was great looking and sweet in her way, and I ached to be with her. But I couldn't help thinking how I was in college now and she was in high school and how they were two different worlds. I still liked her, but love has a way of fading whether you want it to or not.

I returned to Earlham in January feeling less like a wide-eyed freshman than I did in the fall. I was ready to embrace my new life. Plus there was a girl from St. Louis, with straw-blonde hair, a peach complexion and sensuous curves that I had asked out a couple of times. It was time to take make a move.

February 4, 1966 (letter from LH to PB)

Dear Pete

Winter has fallen with a vengeance. We had about 20 inches of snow. It drifted like crazy up to eight feet on the Maryland campus. Most of the rotten stuff is still on the ground, melting into a filthy slush during the day and freezing into sheets of ice during the night. I figure by the time it all melts, Washington will look a lot like Venice. But I'm happy.

Susie came to town last Friday, and because of the blizzard stayed until Tuesday. I would really like to tell you exactly how I feel about her but it is hard. Really I think that I'm in love with her in a sort of detached way. She fills my thoughts, but I know that there are too many things I want to do, too many women I want to screw, and too many places I'd like to visit that prevent me from locking myself up with another person.

We spent three days together—three days of whispered promises of love, of drunken sex and happy shared laughter. It will end soon—probably this summer. But I'm very happy loving her now.

Lorraine Tobin will be attending MJC this semester and I hope I can be of some help to her. Which, in a roundabout way, brings me to the subject of the famous Jay Levy. Jay, I'm saddened to report is sort of rotting away. He does nothing and seems far and distant. He has plans and rejects them or lets them die as soon as they are made. He wanders back and forth looking for I don't know...himself? He's really in bad shape and there isn't anything I can do. He had a good job a few weeks ago at Safeway making $2.30 an hour. He quit after the first day. That incident was the final evidence. Despite myself, I have lost almost all the respect and admiration I once had for him.

He comes here often but is usually hard to talk with and grumpy as only he can be. I sort of pity him and hate myself for it. I can't tell him directly that I think he's a bum, so I suggest jobs and cetera but it doesn't do any good. The very sad-making part of the whole thing is that he knows he's becoming nothing. Last night he said to me: "I'm going downhill." "Fix it," I answered. "Get a job. Move out of the house. Hitchhike around the world. Go to Australia. Do <u>something</u>." He had no reply save for a mumbled grump. I don't know. Perhaps a letter from you would do him some good. However don't let on that I'm telling you what's going on.

No word from the goddamn Peace Corps as of yet but as soon as there is I will send you a telegram. I still want to go but have decided not to drop dead from disappointment if they don't accept me. I have good enough grades to get into Frostburg or Towson, and both of these schools will kindly pay for my tuition. So I'm looking forward to the start of next year with a grin.

Old Robert Ochsman was in our fair suburb last week for a couple of days. He's well, asks for you, is growing a beard, has a 3.5 average, is horny, corny and basically the same old Bob Ochsman. He reminds me of the Rock of Gibraltar with a college degree.

And now, since I haven't heard from you in a month. How the fucking hell are you? Where are the Snowdens of yesteryear? How are your grades and what are is your general outlook? Are you happy? Simply answer the last question with a couple of succinct pages of well-done prose and I'll leave you alone for a while. Tell me what you are doing and when you will be home. Your woman pines for you.
I remain your frantic correspondent.
Larry

It was winter in Indiana, gray, rainy, cold. I felt confined in a room the size of monks' quarters. The walls were closing in. To escape, I joined an intramural basketball team, studied in the library or played hearts at the student center. I made daily rounds from dorm to classroom to cafeteria to mailbox. I took long walks down Highway 40 in search of pizza and love. I found only pizza.

I guess Larry had it right. I was lonely. There were indeed some lovely coeds on campus, but it was a bit like catch and release. I hadn't found anyone I hoped to hook for good—or even for a time.

I found myself hanging out with Roy and Brad who were living in Bundy Hall. It was funkier and rowdier than Barrett. It was no place to study or get a good night's sleep. But I was drawn there.

We talked endlessly about anything going on campus or the lack thereof, and about what we knew about the world from reading Newsweek, Time, Ramparts and the I.F. Stone Weekly.

There was so much to absorb. LBJ said we will be in Vietnam as long as there is communist aggression—whatever that meant. The U.S. had just resumed bombing North Vietnam after a month long pause. Cambodia complained of U.S. and South Vietnamese incursions. Julian Bond was denied his seat in the Georgia legislature because of his opposition to the war. David Miller was sentenced to jail for burning his draft card. An anti-war rally in Manhattan drew a quarter million protesters. Events of great portent swirled all around us as we prepped for mid-term exams.

February 13, 1966 (letter from PB to LH)

Dear Larry,

Open the blasted windows. Let in that bastardly teasing sunshine and damn the wind. I feel good again—having recovered from my first bad cold here at school. I feel like a snake that's just shed a superfluous outer skin. I feel like hollering and why the fuck not? I just aced a goddamn mid-term exam in Problems of Philosophy 12. I also got an equally hot mid-term grade in Intro to Music. It may not last, but my sense of exhilaration will sustain me for the present. And a good thing too because I stumbled back to school—a place, alternatively, of learning and sexual frustration—feeling considerably older and wiser. The glitter of collegiate life had faded. I was more than a little depressed at the thought of spending the next several months walking in circles. Then, out of nowhere, there is this freshman chick who is rapidly becoming enamored with my holy essence.

Barbi- short blonde hair, blue eyes, pert little breasts, and a hell of a nice ass, and sweet. She's the daughter of a Methodist preacher in St Louis. Okay, you are awarded five full minutes to scream, curse, light up a cigarette, scratch your ass or whatever, but I have to say this one is different. For one thing, she's a treat to talk to and who has the kind of intelligence that is sensitive and original and worthwhile and meaningful. I know I sound like I'm in love with her. But don't worry, she hasn't fully penetrated my steely exterior but she provides a hell of a lot to do around here and I don't feel so horny all the time. The crux of the problem is what to do about Sue. S. Advise me. Please.

By the way, I got a letter from Bob. that he wrote while drunk on Gordon's Gin in Chapel Hill, or as he calls it, the land of grits and the Ku Klux Klan, while listening to Monk's Criss-Cross on a new pair of stereo earphones his brother (Moose) sent him on his birthday. He said he had the volume turned up so loud that it would probably make your balls go into a 162.3456 miles semi-elliptical hyperbolic semi-quadratic orbit around nebulae 23. Is that really possible?

I will be getting home on March 18th, which won't even be close to your final exams. It follows that we should jump into Levy's car and head south to see Bob. I can't think of anything I'd rather do than go on a long road trip with the two of you and a pint of good old Jack Daniels and drive into the wind, humming A Summer Song. Make it possible even if it's impossible.

I hope to hell the Peace Corps answers affirmatively. Meanwhile study, I guess.

Pete

February 17, 1966 (letter from LH and Jay to PB)

Your last letter was quite amusing, and Jay and I both were very glad to hear from you. As a matter of fact we agreed that your most recent would be a valuable addition to the collection of Pete's letters that we have been compiling.

As you may or may not know Jay and I have arranged with Random House to publish all your letters to us in a book. Although Mr. Cerf was skeptical about publishing an anthology of such an unusual length, it will come out in early spring. We were wondering whether or not you could arrange to be in town for the autograph party and "Meet the Author" session that we have scheduled for you. It will take place in the men's room of the Library of Congress on April 1st.

Also present will be other minor people that we are sure you don't remember: Milton Berliner, the writer; Mrs. Nancy Berliner, your mother; Kathy Berliner, your sister; Lorraine Tobin, a friend of yours; Sue S., another friend of yours; and of course Jay Levy and myself (Larry Horwitz). It has been such a long time since you have seen either Jay or me (Larry Horwitz) that we are sure you don't recall us. Jay is the tall blond boy who died in his mother's arms at the roulette table at Monte Carlo. You can recognize him by the wooden leg he sports as the result of an encounter with a white whale.

I, Larry Horwitz, am the handsome devil-may-care son of a bitch who was famous during the twenties for constantly defending Ernest Hemingway's honor whenever he got too drunk to fight the various Frenchman he insulted while we were in Paris. I will wear a Legion of Merit pin on my lapel. I'm also easily noticeable by the fact that I smoke cigarettes exactly the way Humphrey Bogart did. If all else fails, we are both in the local telephone book under "People I Used to Know."

However, getting back to the original purpose of the letter, both Mr. Levy and myself, not to mention the folks at Random House, are all atwitter over this exciting new work entitled "Letters from a Pal or in Absentia." Pete we hope you approve. Now both Jay and I have contributed all the letters we have received from you in the past 18 years and, as a stroke of great good fortune, we have prevailed upon Mr. Robert Ochsman, formerly of Silver Spring, now a practicing vivisectionist in Sao Paulo, Brazil, to contribute his letters from you.

After careful editing, we have amassed a remarkable collection of your letters into a volume of three and a half pages of rather large print. We feel that we can get the famous illustrator, Arnold Stang, famous for his work on bathroom walls the world over, to add his talents to our endeavor. Please advise us if there are any additional plans or suggestions you would have.
Cordially,
Larry Horwitz and Jay Levy

Ok, I got it. Sarcasm, they say, is the lowest form of humor. Or was it puns?

February 18, 1966 (letter from LH to PB)

So it is about 8:30 on Thursday evening. I'm in the Silver Spring library sitting like one of Buddha's reincarnations and watching every single girl, woman or female that walks in, feeling like I need a stiff drink. My two philosophy texts are on my lap but I just can't seem to get into the bastards even though I want to. Philosophy is one of my favorite courses. Anyhow I have in my coat pocket a letter to you that I wrote an hour ago in a fit of pique and loneliness. I have enclosed it for your general amusement.

I run out of the library in search of the elusive and oftentimes wonderful sound of Levy's magic personality. He's not home, naturally.

Instead he's working at the new Sears in White Oaks as, of all things, assistant manager of the men's furnishings department.

But where are the Petes of yesteryear? I scream silently into the night. Where's my delectable and oh so sweet and tender Susie who I love so dearly? Where the hell are people I love so much that it hurts? I answer sadly far away and I need them badly.

It's Friday and I have only one class at 3 p.m. I am in the process of cleaning up my room--picking up dirty socks to the strains of Erroll Garner's Concert by the Sea, arranging books while I shake my shaggy head to the music. There is light streaming in the window. When the mail comes, I rush over expecting for some word from the Peace Corps and I find instead your letter.

I open the damn thing and my room was suddenly filled with a burst of yellow and red light while fireworks spelled out in 3,000 different colors the word happiness. I had no recourse but to sit down, light a cigarette. It is a good page and a half of prose that will in all probability sustain me for the next month. I am sure that if I were going to try to repeat Jesus' act of going into the desert for a month without food or water in search of God. I would only need one letter such as this to carry me through the ordeal.

You seek advice my son concerning the sensual and plague-like problem of Sue S. I can tell you without too much mushiness and grandfatherly Pollyannishness that you should without a moment's hesitation (DO NOT PASS GO, DO NOT COLLECT $200) send her packing. I know. I know. Visceral pleasures are fine but for god sake and yours, send her a careless and unemotional farewell.

I am forced to report on one seemingly endless conversation I had with her concerning your silence through the mails. She worries and loves you and is lonely without you and on and on ad nausea. Understand that she is quite capable of choking you to death on sweet but shallow love. She wants to get married and that scares me silly.

Don't for Venus' sake worry about your steely exterior with this little blond from good old East St. Louis. If she is good for you and makes your heart noticeably lighter, and you are good for her and bring a smile to her lips with your antics, then let your goddamn exterior rust.

It is a waste of time, I have found out, to worry about it, and in my erratic and hysterical manner, I have reached some sort of an agreement *with my soul. I have ceased to become sad and somber more than once a week. I try to find excitement and happiness in my work at school and usually succeed. I am meeting new and strangely different people all the time, and (this is my major problem) I can't seem to stop falling in love with everybody on a moment's notice. I think that right this second I would gladly lay down my sword and cape and humility for no less than twelve young femmes. I am worried that I may be slightly mad. However, I have decided that my madness is a helluva lot saner than what generally passes for sanity in this screwed up world.*

One more thing before I fall exhausted from the chair onto the floor. I think that I love this girl, this Barbi, simply because she loves you and makes you happy. I want to see her lovely face and speak with her in my insane way. I want to go to a movie and have a beer with the two of you and my Susie. I want all four of us to jump into my VW and go for a drive and have a picnic. I want, I'm afraid, much too much that is impossible. But still I want all these things and more.

Please be happy and know that I await your return.

Larry

More news from the home front, this time from Jay.

February 23, 1966 (letter from JL to PB)

Somewhere in the upper range of a G flat diminished 9th chord

Peterberliner

How are you? I am fine. Something happened. It blew my mind. I finally made my piano playing debut at the Playboy Club in Baltimore last Saturday night at approximately 1:30 a.m.

Lorraine and I were sitting around at the piano bar, and between numbers I was talking to Jimmy Wells (of the Jimmy Wells Trio) about musicians, gigs and jazz in general. Well right after he got finished playing Sonny Rollins' St. Thomas he got up and said listen man come on up and play something. I quickly regained consciousness and took over behind this huge Steinway grand concert job.

At first I was rather feverish but all of a sudden I just started playing without even looking at the bass player or the drummer. I started down that progression of block chords in the intro to When Sunny Gets Blue and took off on the most wonderful trip I could ever hope to take. Christ was it ever great. The sidemen were fantastic and I swear I really lost consciousness again only this time in the swelling wake of harmonies that I was creating.

We shot through 12 bars. Some I played straight, some I gave to the bass (it was easy) and some became all mine. In less than no time it was over. (I smartly ended with a combination of F chord triads with the left hand and it G chord triad with the right), and people there gave me this really damn nice hand and old Jimmy Wells introduces me and everything. Then Wells asked me to stay up there and do another. But at that time I just couldn't because I was just too damn excited or something. Sheet! I surely wish to hell I would have done another number now, but that's how it goes. After they knocked off for the night, I talked to him and made plans to see him at a Sunday afternoon session he would be playing later that day. He's really a vibe player but he does alright on piano.

I went over to Larry's to take him along to the session, only a terrible thing happened just as we were leaving his house. My mother called and told me some pretty bad news. It seems like just that morning that the pawn shop was broken into by some bastards who knocked a damn hole in the wall. So I put off the jam session and shot down to the shop. Well those bastards did alright. I guess they got about 600 rings and watches valued at about nine thousand dollars. They were worth about $14,000 retail. It certainly was one hell of a loss to say the least. It's sort of made everyone around here sick for a while. I doubt that we will ever see those watches and rings again.

School is going pretty damn well, and I have managed to get deferred from going to basic training for the god damn army until I complete the first year. So when I'm out of school this June, I will probably put myself on 24 hours' notice and get the damn basic over with so I'll be back for school again in February.

Larry and I are thinking about getting this apartment in Takoma Park about 3 blocks from school. The rent is only 75 bucks a month but then again you should see the place. The architecture is early 20th century ramshackle. Larry seems to be fairly eager to leave home. On the other hand I sit around trying to figure out life. I suppose I'm spoiled and a taste of poverty would be the perfect panacea to rid me of this gout. I'm still considering, and so far no decision has been made. Naturally I will notify you if I move. The real problem is that the apartment is up 20 stairs, and we can't figure out how to get my piano up there. I don't know what to about it. You know, like I can't go home every day to play it. I leave you with this today by Thomas Parke D'Invilliers only because I like it immensely.

> Then wear the gold hat, if it will move her. If you can bounce
> high, bounce high for her 'til she cries: Lover, gold hatted,
> high bouncing lover, I must have you!

Jay Levy

The vision of Jay playing alongside such a bona fide musician is more than I could have imagined. Plus it was rare to hear him speak so optimistically. Moving out from home? School going well? Too much to expect. Of course the whole thing about the army was troublesome. Then a few days later, I found this letter in my mailbox. It was unsigned but clearly from Jay.

February 27, 1966

I am 20 years old and a student at a junior college in a prominent country in the Western Hemisphere. I live day to day without a single goal in life. There are thousands of things to do, thousands of opportunities available, places to go and see; yet all I do is exist. I am terribly confused about why I'm here (that is on this planet known as Earth) I'm plagued constantly by this question: Would it matter if I were dead or not? Truthfully I cannot think it honestly would. It seems to me that death is one of those things which people always accept one way or the other. That is, people live and die, and when they die they often affect people close to them (friends etc.) but I realize that after a length of time the deceased will fade from the memory, causing little if any anxiety. I certainly would feel uncomfortable about causing this anxiety (providing this is a question in the case of ones close to me) but like I said, I would be only short-term discomfort, from which I feel confident all those concerned would quickly recover. In this country where I reside, the taking of one's life is thought to be a sacrilege and more importantly taking the cowardly way out. Insofar as it has been the cowardly way out, I must disagree. And so far as it being a sacrilege, I'm afraid that could not concern me less, because I do not feel any ties or beliefs in my own or in any other religion. As for as the question of the self-inflicted death being a cowardly way out from the problems of life, my only comment is why should it matter? So early death is death. The cause of death, as much as able, should be left to the individual. I do not see death as an eternal peaceful sleep nor as an adventure in heaven, but rather as an abrupt end. Death is final. Death is the true end. A situation is bad. One is unhappy, and after a reasonable amount of time devoted to thought on the problem and found no other answers, turns to death, not so much as the easiest way out, but as the only way to avoid a life of discontent. I'm upset with myself. I simply do not understand human life as it is here in this country in the Western Hemisphere. I often long to be one of the lower animals and not have the ability to think abstractly or communicate. My hair is growing long. So far I have not been able to have it cut in the usual way. I can feel my hair growing out of my skull, and during times of intense concentration, I can actually hear the hair scrape against the pores of my scalp as it emerges in curly extensions from my brain to survey the situation surrounding my head. I feel cutting it will somehow dull my senses. I love water. I'm simply mad about it. It must be cold and clear. I'm not sure but I think water is connected to my hair. I think my hair is dehydrating me. Its growth is absorbing all my natural body fluid, thus the need for water is constant. This does not bother me for like I said I love the fluid flowing down my throat till I'm bloated and nearly in pain. HELP (scrawled in blue ink)

I read it over about ten times. It was plaintive and disturbing. I feared that something terrible was about to happen. I was clueless as to what to do. I showed the letter to one of the upper class psych majors in my dorm, who read it carefully and said, "Yeah. He sounds pretty fucked up. It's nicely conceived and written though." *Really. I seek your expertise in the human brain and you give me literary criticism?* I dialed his home and got his mother, Ruth. Jay's not home. I haven't seen him in a while, she told me after some pleasantries. Should I tell her I think he's about to jump of a bridge? "Just let him know I called." I called Larry but got no answer. I was pretty sure that he or Larry or Cooper or both were with him talking him down from a ledge. I wrote him a letter. When I went to send it, I found a postcard in my mailbox that said, "*Disregard my last note I was drunk or something.*"

I came home at the end of March for a short break. Happily, Jay was still alive, his mind was intact. I spent several happy hours listening to him work out a couple of tracks from a Vince Guaraldi album. Then we tried to parse the mysteries of Coltrane's *A Love Supreme*, confident that it contained the answers to all of life's questions.

In other rooms and other places, all kinds of music was being played. The pop scene was confusing and contradictory—a random mix of soul and doo-wop; surf songs, folk, and rock. Stevie Wonder, Diana Ross, Jan and Dean, the Monkees and the Mamas and Papas. The Beatles were concocting *Yellow Submarine* and the Rolling Stones were recording *Paint it Black*. Barry Sadler crooned the *Ballad* of the *Green Berets* while Phil Ochs sang *I Ain't Marching Any More*. It was hard to make sense of it all. Give me jazz, timeless and transcendent, any day.

April 6, 1966 (letter from PB to LH)

Dear Larry,

It seems odd in retrospect that I last saw you, and said goodbye for another two months, in such a drunken stupor after a thoroughly enjoyable evening at Barslaag's, in which I recall for the first time allowing myself to exit reality for a short sojourn from reality only to rediscover in his living room chair, a box of Cheerios, and an unsteady fire of screen images of time and space. You see it was there that I wanted time to stop.

I was very sad, amused and almost happy reading your letter. It is too damn bad about the Peace Corps. I figure that after drowning yourself in alcohol, you might want to stomp out into the night wearing a John Glenn tee shirt and a pair of jack boots and conduct a retaliatory raid in which you steal some of President Johnson's autograph pens or the District Commissioner's license plate in retaliation.

Alternatively, you could get a goddamn college catalog and look for a college to go to (after getting straight A's this term). There are a lot of amazing places out there and the fact is that all schools give scholarships and or work-study grants and loans. Besides, I happen to know that your old man has millions stashed away.

Up here, most of us are saving the Peace Corps for when we don't get into graduate school — and our student deferments run out. Anyway what makes me happy is that this is going to be a productive summer —perhaps one spent writing, reading, fucking and drinking, not too much riding around going nowhere but actually going places.

Will write again.

Pete

It was spring. Indiana was delightfully sunny and bright. Barbi and I were enjoying the afterglow. Being together seemed comfortably light and unburdened. She had a blithe Midwestern sparkle, and she laughed a lot. She was smart and well-read, and very much my match. Back home, Larry was also welcoming the change in seasons.

April 15, 1966 (letter from LH to PB)

Pete,

I'm sitting here in my brown and yellow green front yard looking for all the world like a guy in a Gant shirt ad in the New Yorker and letting the bubbling squint-making sunshine wash all over my youthful countenance. In short I simply feel like using my amazing creativity in some way and a letter to you seems like the best way right now. It's Friday and I have no classes today. I'm passing my time reflecting on my life and those lives that I influence. I find myself moving in several spheres. Each is different and separate. There is a certain amount of overlap but, in essence, I exist as a slightly different person for several varied groups. It interests increasingly.

Susie was in town this week staying with a girlfriend and devoting her evenings to me. We spent Tuesday night at rehearsal after which we clutched and groped in the darkness of my father's immense and comfortable new Ford with its optional bedroom front bench seat. We parked next to a local elementary school. It was raining, and she thought that was terrible. Her beauty is magnified to me by about a million fold when she says things like, "Larry, we can't park here at an elementary school." and being the crass, insensitive bastard that I am, I answer, "Bullshit. C'mere."

The next night, we went to dinner at the Charcoal Hearth and then sped through the rain to Rockville where my cousin Buzzy lives. I had asked and he had consented to let me use his apartment. I had my own key and walked in like a stud, made a couple of drinks, slipped on some mood music, made some nifty repartee, and asked the fatal question. Again that little high school girl threw me into catastrophic throes of alternating love and confusion.

"Larry, what do you mean when you ask me to go to bed with you? Does that include all the nuances and rituals or can we just go to bed together."

As you might guess, we wound up in the sack thrashing around in a series of abortive movements known as "heavy necking." Actually that stuff is foreplay and without it's a logical conclusion you feel like Maury Wills quivering off of third base with the winning run and watching the next three batters strike out in slow motion.

A careful re reading of my first paragraph makes me wonder if I would not better serve the world as a pasta cook rather than a writer of the GREAT AMERICAN NOVEL. Jesus Christ on a Schwinn bicycle wearing a fedora and playing snatches of When the Saints Go Marching In on a shiny pocket cornet could not thrill me the way this spring (SPRING) does. Colors, I have just realized, are much more vivid and alive seen in the amazing sunlight that occurs in April, May and early June. From my position I can see fresh red blossoms popping up everywhere. I can see daffodils that are so yellow they burn. I can see the sky (blue and purple) filled with cotton clouds moving sleepily in the breeze. Today I wish to take a James Audubon—Isaac Walton—Henry David Thoreau attitude about the whole scene.
Don't get hung up in a riff.
Larry

The close of my first year in college was nearing. Dick, who was about to graduate, had resolved the draft conundrum by signing up to work for the International Voluntary Service. It came with a two-year deferment. But he didn't do it to avoid Vietnam. That was exactly where he was headed. My parents were not happy, knowing they would face two years of anxiety while their elder son was in a war zone.

May 9, 1966 (letter from LH to PB)

A mournful Tuesday Night. Tired. Blue. Awake and eyes smoke bleary from cornea to lash. Writing another episode to a memory of a real friend, far and away. You too I think, a little lost.

Family strife. And tears streaming down my mother's wrinkled and beautiful face. My father, cruel ogre, yelling and seeking and explaining and telling his refrain of lies. I sit wondering about it all and try to keep some modicum of happiness flowing through my blood stream at all times. But I'm sad. And sick. I will, someday, vomit it all up, then brush my teeth with love. The time is long overdue. I must get out. And away. And be happy. Reading, I want you to know, much of the existentialists. Soren Kierkegaard. Holy, faithful man. Herr Nietzsche. Scary, strongman. Very muscular. Jean-Paul Sartre. With glasses on, an intellectual. But not a bore.

I also am learning about the nervous system of the frog. And always remember, a frog does have teeth. Why? I venture an opinion. No one ever solved a single emotional hang-up with that knowledge.

Bob Ochsman will be wealthy. You and I won't. Levy will never be very happy. I will. I love too much. You don't love loudly enough. So I am reminded of a picture and a story of Barbie. Fresh young girl. Who makes you want to do certain things. Has your young man's fancy turned to thoughts of love now that it is spring?

Susi on the telephone tonight. I asked her to marry me. She refused. However she said that she has made other, better decisions. I gather now she will let me. Sober. With the right attitude. And a rubber. I want her to let me do it in the light. But I'm a pig. Also sensitive.

I'm very frightened that no one will be happy. I know people now that are dead inside. But they are only eighteen. I want to be five years old for another ten years. I wish I were a Buddhist. I wish I were a turtle that could think, sort of a Kafka creation. I'd wear glasses and read by the woodland light and eat a gnat or two. But I would never talk to people. Or they to me. Some little child, eyes wonder-wide, would bring me home. And he'd have a fantastic library with all of the Greek classics. I don't want to be like a person in Eliot's "Wasteland." Neither do I really want to turn into a Hemingway. Myself is all.

Where the hell are you? Please find time to tell me your thoughts. I love the story of the river but I want to know more what goes through your head when you have a headache. Or are sitting on a toilet. I'm in a very bad, sad mood. I hope we will one day share a pint or two and talk of recent accomplishments. I will sleep soundly as soon as I scream at you to read *The Ginger Man* which will cause you to understand the fecal matter above much better. I yearn to see and sense you again. I am still heterogeneous.

HORWITZ

May 14, 1966 (letter from PB to LH)

Larry,

I got your past couple of letters but I didn't write back mainly because I have humanities papers up the ass. But to give you an idea of what floats and dances across my angular mind as I walk around campus, it goes something like this. I'm thinking a lot about coming home. And about summer and drinking beer and eating steaks we cook in one of our backyards. I'm think about talking about jazz and books and sex and carburetors and about how drinking isn't the quite the same here because, if you want to know the truth, you're lucky if you even know more than three people you really enjoy drinking with, especially knowing that everyone I really know and enjoy is back in Silver Spring.

About the Newport Jazz Festival. It has a fantastic line up. Tickets will run us about $20. It goes from July 1st to the 4th. It's an eight hour drive from home and may depend on whether I can get the time off.

Also, what I want to do is convince whoever we have to that the two of us should take about three weeks off at the end of the summer, taking maybe a couple of sleeping bags and some walking boots, and hitchhike to Colorado City in Texas, to see Tex and his quarter horses, and his family's 128,000 acre spread. He's said he will drive us into Mexico, and we can hitchhike through steamy Southern towns and still get back in time for school.

The other day I sent a note to Sue S. which made me feel better. I didn't say much but then again I didn't intend to. She wrote back and had a number of interesting things to report. Like Jay has been asking her out. Also, it appears that the ultimate goal in life for everyone in Silver Spring is to get their hands on acid and grass (or, alternatively, on grass and acid). She also said that you got a motorcycle? These things require further discussion.

From reading the letter, I feel like I'm crazy about her. The problem is that I get crazy about a lot of chicks but never for too damn long. Anyway I don't feel like diving into that particular dung heap of emotional trivia. I'm sick of relationships. I want only to hear music, eat grapes from the vine and be creative as possible. This will be an important summer for me for writing. I've seen many things, heard many things and felt still more. I doubt if I will ever take LSD because I sense I'm potentially imbalanced as it is, and more, importantly, I have eyes and heart to make colors as bright as I can stand them and also gray, which is probably the way this letter sounds. I want to hear you lie a little bit and to hear Jay be the wild and hugely funny person I know him as.

When I write to you, I feel some sort of weird melancholia, but truthfully, I could tell you about a hundred things that have made me laugh out loud in the last couple of days-- but that can wait. Be patient.
Pete

Classes were over, but I stayed to watch Dick graduate. Barbi and I had been together all spring. I planned to meet her after her last work shift for Saga Foods and share a tender farewell. But before that I went to Dick's house and drank several bottles of Schlitz. By the time we met, I was three sheets to the wind. The horizon was spinning.

"This is the last time we're together," I uttered dolefully.

"Actually, I'm not leaving until Sunday."

"You mean we can say goodbye tomorrow?"

"Yes."

"That's great," I said and staggered back to my dorm alone.

We parted the next day. I knew that whatever we had together had run its course. Not that I said anything at the time. No sense dealing with it then if I could put it off to another day—or avoid it completely. *Did that make me a jerk?*

Chapter 7

Summer in the City

Dad had arranged a summer job for me as a copy boy at the Washington Daily News. I started a few days after I got home. I would earn a buck twenty-five an hour running errands for the reporters, but I hoped to write a story or two in the course of the summer.

Dad's career as a reporter often put him at the center of history. At a press conference about charges of wartime corruption levied at Howard Hughes, Dad asked, *"Are you saying that you had only 1% of the contracts, but you are getting 100% of the investigation?"* Hughes replied, "Exactly." The next day the phrase, attributed directly to Hughes, appeared in headlines around the world.

In the 1950s, he covered the Senate hearings in which Joe McCarthy tried to find a communist in every corner. Dad went to all the national political conventions. On election nights, he stayed up until dawn writing stories about who won and lost and why.

In addition to reporting, Dad wrote a weekly column he called Capitol Punishment. He was also the paper's music critic and reviewed concerts by the National Symphony Orchestra and other performances. Sometimes he took me along to see virtuosos like Andres Segovia, Pablo Casals, Andre Watts and Van Cliburn from our aisle seats in the second or third row. As soon as the concert was over, we leapt up and rushed to the News so Dad could write up his notes. I plundered the vending machine and waited until he was done. We usually got home around midnight.

On December 5, 1950, Dad and the Washington Post's critic, Paul Hume, covered a concert at Constitution Hall given by Margaret Truman—the president's daughter. Hume's review read:

> *Miss Truman is a unique American phenomenon with a pleasant voice of little size and fair quality. She is extremely attractive on stage. Yet Miss Truman cannot sing very well. She is flat a good deal of the time and more so last night than at any time we have heard her in past years.*

These comments did not sit well with the President who let Hume know about it. Hume was going to bury the President's response, but before he did he shared it with Dad. The next day, it appeared in the News.

H.S.T. (Hello Sweet Thing)

Mr. Hume,

> *I've just read your lousy review of Margaret's concert. I've come to the conclusion that you are an "eight ulcer man on four ulcer pay."*
>
> *It seems to me that you are a frustrated old man who wishes he could have been successful. When you write such poppy-cock as was in the back section of the paper you work for it shows conclusively that you're off the beam and at least four of your ulcers are at work.*
>
> *Someday I hope to meet you. When that happens you'll need a new nose, a lot of beefsteak for black eyes, and perhaps a supporter below! Westbrook Pegler, a gutter snipe, is a gentleman alongside you. I hope you'll accept that statement as a worse insult than a reflection on your ancestry.*

H.S.T.

The story was picked up by the wire services and reprinted everywhere.

Dad was a gifted reporter. His political stories and music reviews could be both insightful and entertaining. My favorite review was his shortest:

Liberace last night, at a concert at Constitution Hall, demonstrated his versatility by playing the black keys as well as the white.

Every morning, I dressed in a sports coat and tie, and arrived for work dripping with sweat. That was D.C. for you. Up an hour and I already wished I could take another shower. The News was in a six-story granite building at 14th and K. I worked on the fourth floor in a cavernous news room with long wooden tables for the reporters, oak desks for the editors and glass-walled offices for the management. On the tables and desks sat ponderous steel typewriters. Strewn among them were stacks of newspapers, shreds of carbon-backed yellow paper torn from the wire services printers that hummed in the background, piles of typing paper, fat yellow pencils, and paste-pots of rubber cement. Next to each typewriter was a bulky black rotary-dial telephone.

At times, I worked the early shift from four a.m. to noon. The only one there when I arrived was the night editor, a curmudgeonly journalist who let me write obituaries. This required culling through the notes taken from families that had called the day before. The News got a lot of calls from families directly, particularly from African American families because the News was the one newspaper in town that covered the community. Sometimes it meant taking a cab to the family's home to get a photo or a quote. It was a somber and awkward task. But I relished seeing the words I had written in the newspaper later that day.

When the editor finished doctoring a story and writing a headline, he called me over. I stuffed in in a glass cartridge and sent it through the pneumatic tube to the floor below where they were typed into linotype machine produced letters and punctuation marks out of molten lead. After all the headlines and stories were set up, the presses would churn out a quarter million newspapers at lightning speed. The first edition hit the streets at noon. The last was delivered by paper boys to homes in the city and suburbs, including ours, by 5 p.m.

The reporters and editors on the day shift arrived around nine. The phones rang. The reporters bantered. The editors barked orders. The typewriters clattered as reporters rushed to write late-breaking stories for the next edition. Soon the tables and desks were littered with coffee cups and ashtrays that were overflowing with half-smoked cigarettes.

Dad began his day by drinking a cup of coffee and talking to the other reporters. He did a quick scan of the wires—AP, UPI and Reuters. He glanced through the Post, the Star, and the New York Times, then left to go to the Senate Press Gallery at the Capitol, from which he covered hearings and floor debates.

After working my shift, I got home in time to nap in the afternoon heat. With no air-conditioning, our house sometimes felt like a furnace. After dinner was over and the dishes were done, I called Larry or Jay or Bob to figure out what we would do that evening. We never planned stuff with Cooper. He either appeared or he didn't. We left it to fate.

I was 18, old enough to buy or be served beer or wine in D.C. (but not in Maryland). A healthy part of my meager paycheck was squandered in bars or jazz joints, or the liquor store just over the District line. Sometimes we went to jazz clubs, the Cellar Door, Bohemian Caverns or Blues Alley, to see jazz giants like Dizzy Gillespie, Thelonius Monk and Charlie Byrd.

One night, Louis Armstrong and Ella Fitzgerald were performing at Carter-Barron, an outdoor venue in Rock Creek Park. We didn't have tickets, so we ended up climbing over a chain link fence to get in. We crept through the woods, military style, to where we could see the stage from the shadows of the trees. When they sang, *"Let's Do It—Let's Fall in Love,"* we applauded wildly along with the paying customers.

Another time, we drove to Shady Grove to see the Dave Brubeck Quartet. *Time Out* and *Time Further Out* had sold over a million copies, and *Take Five* was high on the charts. We got there early. As we walked from the parking lot, Jay asked "Isn't that Paul Desmond sitting over there in that Chevy?"

"Yeah. It has to be."

"I'm going over there right now to tell him how much I dig his music," Jay said.

Shady Grove held only a couple thousand people. We had good seats and were anxious for the concert to begin. Once they started, they played for about two hours. I couldn't get enough.

When the music ended, we didn't want to leave. We hung around as they talked to fans. Somebody asked Joe Morello how he got so much speed in his drum rolls.

"It's all in the wrist," he said, and showed him on his drum kit which he was in the process of taking apart.

"But you must be getting a lot of ricochet off the head," the fan said.

"Not really," Joe said and proceeded to drum at an equally mind-boggling pace on a padded stool.

It was getting really late. Morello was still packing up and we offered to help. Suddenly, I was carrying his snare drum through the rain to the back of an Oldsmobile station wagon. I was as careful as I could be because it felt to me like a sacred object.

On other nights, we went to Dupont Circle, a hang-out for hipsters and folkies and artists. There were always people strumming guitars, hitting bongos, and talking about politics. It was one of the rare places for inter-racial socializing which added to its allure.

Nearby there were the Circle and the Janus movie theaters that showed films that rarely made it to the suburbs. There were restaurants, coffee houses and book stores. The Phillips Gallery was a couple of blocks away.

One particularly humid evening, we were sitting on a bench expecting Cooper to show at any minute. Dupont Circle. It felt like *Waiting for Godot*. He had told Larry that he had obtained some grass and would bring it to us there. When he finally showed, we gave him ten bucks, and he gave us a plastic bag stuffed with seeds, stems and a few dried leaves. Before trying it, we went to an Irish bar that Larry liked. It was crowded and noisy with conversation that sounded like the jabber of parakeets. Larry and Bob grabbed a table. I went to the bar to get a pitcher of Guinness. As I waited I was approached by a blonde in a short skirt and leather boots— more Georgetown than Dupont Circle. I was surprised to see that it was Phyllis Duvall. The last time I had seen her was at our high school graduation.

Phyllis was looking very stylish. She seemed more mature than when I had last seen her. I guess we all were. Even one year in college had an effect. Now we were old enough to drink and old enough to fight a war. Just not old enough to vote.

She was as fresh and sweet as ever. As Larry once said, "The thing about Phyllis Duvall is that she always looks like she just stepped out of a hot shower."

"Hi. You look fantastic!" I said. It wasn't a come-on. I couldn't help myself.

She blushed a bit, although I may have imagined it since the lighting was pretty dim.

"I knew you were in town," she said.

"You must have ESP."

She laughed and said, "I saw one of your stories in the News. We get it at home. The Agatha Christie one. I told my mother that you were a famous reporter I knew from high school. She was impressed."

"The *ABC Murders*. I'm amazed you saw it. I've only written about three stories. Most of the time, I'm just a go-fer."

My pitcher came. Phyllis looked toward a table where there was a girl with long black hair and a couple arty types-- skinny guys who look liked they hadn't bathed in a while.

"I gotta go," she said. "Good to see you." Then she added, "You should come by sometime."

"I will."

Meet the Beatles

By the end of the summer, I had written a bunch of obituaries and two movie reviews. I wrote a story about the Erroll Garner and Lou Rawls concert at Carter-Barron and rewrote some press releases about shopping mall openings and the like. But then came the assignment of a lifetime, when the city editor called me and Pat Collins to his desk.

"I have something for you boys," he said, "because you are probably the only ones who give a shit about the Beatles. I need you to go down to a press conference they're holding today at DC Stadium and cover their concert tonight."

"We can handle that sir," Pat said earnestly.

The Beatles burst into our consciousness in 1964, with catchy pop tunes that, in truth, we kind of scoffed at. At the time, we were listening to jazz virtuosos. How could Ringo Starr compare to Philly Jo Jones? Clearly, these four guys were riding their shtick—long hair, tight suits, and bouncy lyrics. But anyone who saw *A Hard Day's Night*, could see they were unique. Then *Help* came out in 1965. It was funny, outrageous, and like the Beatles themselves, irresistible.

The Beatles had the world's attention. Earlier that year, there were stories out that John Lennon had told a reporter that the Beatles were more popular than Jesus. What he actually said was, "Christianity will go. It will vanish and shrink. I needn't argue about that. I'm right and I'll be proved right. We're more popular than Jesus now; I don't know which will go first—rock 'n' roll or Christianity. Jesus was all right but his disciples were thick and ordinary. It's them twisting it that ruins it for me." This caused a lot of people to go nuts. In fact, before their concert in D.C., the local members of the Ku Klux Klan *(Maryland had a KKK?)*, paraded in white robes outside the stadium in protest.

The locker room at D.C. Stadium was packed with reporters and cameramen. Most were there because of the controversy. I didn't care about that. I was just thrilled to see them up close, making fun of themselves and everyone else. They were quick, funny and smart.

By the start of the concert, 32,000 fans, most of them young girls, were bristling with anticipation. A cyclone of screams exploded as the Beatles made their way to the stage in the middle of the diamond and did not subside at until the Beatles left the stadium. They ripped through their playlist (including *Day Tripper, I Wanna Be Your Man, Nowhere Man, Paperback Writer and Long Tall Sally*) in 30 minutes flat. Not that anyone could distinguish the songs they were singing amidst all the shrieking.

Our story appeared in the News the next day.

Beatles Concert: Noisy but Orderly

By Pat Collins and Pete Berliner

"Yesterday all my troubles seemed so far away/Now I need a place to hide away. I said something wrong. Now I long for yesterday."

Paul McCartney and his Beatles crooned the tune into a microphone setup on a stand over second base in the DC Stadium last night, drowned out by a screaming crowd of 30,000 or more, mostly teenagers.

Their fans were just as dedicated as they were back in February 1964 when a mere 5,000 of them at the Coliseum managed to drown out the Beatles first Washington concert.

Charge!

Last night's crowd however was under much better control. Only one fan, a husky youth, leaped from his box seat and managed to outflank the 75 policemen lining the infield from 3rd base around home plate to first base. The boy climbed onto the stage where he danced around Paul, George Harrison, and John Lennon, touching them reverently before police dragged him off.

Meet the Press

The Beatles took these incidents in stride, as they did the questions of newsmen at a press conference in the Senators locker room just before the concert.

"No, we are not planning to break up but it has to happen sometime. Everyone has to progress," Paul *explained.*

Are you planning to write a book of children's stories?

"I'm writing stories but they don't always turn out like children's stories," said John.

Do you regret what you said about being more popular than Jesus and do you think the incident is over?

"It's not over yet," said John. "Not as many people are as upset as I was led to believe."

"What is the greatest drawback of being a Beatle?

"The temptation to say things you shouldn't," said John.

"What do you think of Prime Minister Wilson's economic stabilization policy?"

"I don't think much of it at all," said John.

"Would you comment on trends in your music?

"I've always been interested in Indian music," said George.

Ringo Starr, who'd been listening sleepily, finally got a question. "What are you going to name your next son?"

After a long pause he replied, "I don't know. It might be a girl."

I was about to go back to Earlham for the fall semester when Larry and I went over to see Phyllis. With no semblance of a plan, we knocked on her front door, and she opened it.

"What do you think about hanging out with us tonight?" I asked.

She told us to wait and closed the door. We heard muffled voices from inside. It sounded like an argument. The door flung open, and Phyllis flew by us to Larry's car. Later I learned she was waiting for her date to arrive and told her mother to give him her regrets.

"Where do you want to go," I asked.

"I don't really care," she said. "Just drive."

Our evening suddenly became infinitely more interesting. We cruised. We stopped for burgers and shakes at the Hot

Shoppe. Then we caught up with Bob and some other friends who were on their way to the Ochman's farm in Damascus. Someone brought beer. We drank it as the evening cooled. After a while, Phyllis and I found our way to the barn and sat down in the straw. We breathed the sweet fragrance of alfalfa, leather saddles, and horses. In the quiet and dark, we leaned toward each other and we kissed. I don't recall what she wore or what we said, but I remember the feel of her skin, smooth and warm, how her hair smelled of jasmine and that she tasted like peppermint tea. It felt like something irrevocable was about to happen.

"We really should be together, you know." I insisted.

"I don't think so," she said. It wasn't what I expected her to say.

"Why not?"

"Because you will vanish."

"No I won't."

"Yes you will. When are you going back to school?

"Tomorrow."

"My point exactly."

The next thing we knew there was a commotion. Everyone was leaving. Larry yelled out to say that he was about to go and that it would be a long walk home. When we came out of the barn, I saw him watching as I brushed straw off her back.

It was a long ride home. We were quiet most of the way. When we arrived at the house, I walked her to the door.

"I guess this is it," I said.

"Oh, I'm sure we'll meet again."

"When?"

She leaned closer and whispered. "When the time is right."

"I can live with that," I said but suddenly I wasn't so sure. "I'll miss you, you know."

"Why?" she asked.

"Because you are pretty and smart. And, as I remember from our Composition class, you're a helluva good writer."

"You sure know how to make a girl feel good."

"Should I go on?"

"No. That'll do."

We kissed goodbye. I held onto her for a long time. Then she slipped through the door. I walked back to the car, already feeling regret.

Chapter 8

At the beginning of sophomore year, I moved into a room in Bundy Hall with Brad and Roy. Brad was from Glastonbury, Connecticut. Before coming to Earlham, he had been at an exclusive prep school back east called The Gunnery. He smoked a briar pipe. He was bawdy, cynical and self-deprecating. Roy was from Shaker Heights near Cleveland. His dad was a solid Republican and a businessman. Roy was blond-haired, optimistic, and a good guy. All through freshman year, he was impeccably clad. He wore ironed shirts, color-coordinated slacks and socks, and polished loafers. Later, riding the Cultural Revolution, he limited his attire to seldom-washed blue jeans, blue work shirts and ragged tennis shoes—bravely striking a blow against the Empire.

If I were to compare them to the *Odd Couple*, Roy would be *Felix* to Brad's *Oscar*. This was particularly evident after Roy lost one of his contacts, which were costly to replace. Roy reverted to wearing glasses. He was really happy the next day when Brad yelled at him from the bathroom down the hall and said, "Roy, I have your contact."

"Really? Where did you find it?"

"On the end of my dick."

It was true. Roy must have dropped it from his eye when climbing onto the upper bunk. It fell into the pair of underwear that was lying on the floor. Eschewing a clean pair, Brad put on the ones he wore the day before, hence the transfer of the contact. Roy soaked it in solution for two days before he put it back in his eye.

It was time to declare our majors. I had decided on English because I liked to read. I also aspired to a deeper understanding of literature. By luck, I got into a Contemporary Lit class taught by a young professor named Paul Lacey. He was somewhat pear-shaped, prematurely gray, persistently good-humored, and frequently appeared in plaid sport jackets, striped shirts, and checkered ties that were severely at odds with each other. When lecturing, he seemed to be lounging, and he was brilliant without being pedantic.

October 11, 1966 (letter from LH to PB)

Bang. The goddamn sun is shining again and, you know, I'm wearing faded jeans and my good old flappy flannel shirt, my pockets full of pens, glasses, lighter, and cigarettes. And there are these colors and these leaves and it's October which causes eye-squinting happiness and, as per usual, I'm sniffing around young blonde color-coordinated ethereal-girl Phyllis Duvall who is naturally confusing the shit out of me. We sit under this big wide leafy friendly tree next to the cafeteria. Her pale-stocking legs tucked under herself. We're lounging around there on the grass and fallen leaves and all. How cute, man, how utterly campusy and American and junior collegiate!

I don't have too many thoughts at a time like that except, phonily: "What can I say or do now that will really, you know, slay this warm little chickeepoo?" I mean, what knock-out Salinger-like utterance will woo and win this darling little sex ball of a hippie, huh?

And she, in all innocence, asks, "Have you heard from Pete Berliner."

Gawddam and sheet. This causes a crotch twitch and a sour taste behind my teen for two reasons: One (1): Why in the living hell have I not, indeed, heard from you yet? And two (2) Why oh why is this little image of Dupont Circle, Georgetown, Brentano's and underground flicks <u>still</u> interested in your gay but absent asshole? Why? Why? Jesus H Christ…as if she doesn't tell me, soon enough, exactly why.

"I wish Pete went to school around here," says Phyllis.

"Why?" Says me.   "Cause he certainly is a sight for sore eyes, for crying out loud," says Phyllis.

So I laugh a very forced laugh in order to mask a noise that sounds very much like gnashed teeth and say, "Whaaat?" and she puts the old cherry on the butterscotch man with this little jewel, "He has a neat face. It's curly. Pete has a curly face."

To tell you the truth, that was not exactly what I was hoping to hear. That said, I'm more concerned with you at the present time. I suppose I could offer all sorts of shuffle-my-feet-grin-like-an-ass-Pete-Berliner type excuses for why you haven't written and I've come up with a few if you need them. Like you lost our typewriter. Or had your writing hand amputated due to a serious error on the part of the Biology Department. Or you've been struck blind by love, lightning, god's wrath or non-stop studying. Or maybe you just don't feel particularly like dashing off anything cause it takes too much time and makes you think of endless summers and suspended friendships and absent talks and hazy memories of Levy's piano and Bob's pimples and my whatever and whomever.

> *A cold sadness was there. He had spoken of himself, of his loneliness which he feared. Of whom are you speaking? Stephen asked at length. Cranly did not answer.—Portrait of an Artist as a Young Man*

Whatever goes on, I understand. Write when you feel the need and the muse is in your silly head.

Larry

I was surprised only slightly that barely a month after I left Phyllis' embrace, Larry was following her around like a randy Pekinese. *Was there no honor among friends?* Of course, I had no claim on Phyllis, but it was disquieting.

Jay came to visit me at Earlham as a prelude to boot camp. That was a shock. Jay was the last person I could imagine wearing a uniform. I couldn't recall ever seeing the slightest wrinkle in his Brooks Brothers slacks. It was hard to envision him in fatigues, crawling through the mud while live ammunition was sprayed above his head. He reminded me that he was only joining Reserves, and there was zero chance that he would be shipped abroad.

I was trying to understand why he had enlisted. College students were deferred from the draft as long as they maintained a C average. How hard could that be? But somehow Jay had let his slide underwater, even while knowing that colleges were required to report that to the local draft board, which was located just across the street. At that point, a cousin suggested that he join him in enlisting in the Army Reserve Postal Unit. The worse that could happen would be throwing out a shoulder while slinging envelopes into the proper slots.

Reserves or not, he would still have to go to basic training, as well as weekend drills and summer camps. But for the most part, he would be at home.

Jay stayed in my dorm from Friday until Sunday. Then he disappeared like a whirlwind bounding into the sky. Everything that was upside down and crazy when he was here, reverted to the norm. We went back to going to class, reading books, writing papers and grinding our way through academics. We heard from him soon after his visit.

October 27, 1966 (letter from JL to PB)

Happiness definitely comes in on tiptoes. I've just arrived home from a most enjoyable airplane ride. I'm full of wonderful memories which whirl through my inhaling nostrils. I'm so damn happy to see you out there in the land of flatness and chill that all I can really say is "Crepuscule"! Think of one. If I Were a Bell. That Lady is a Tramp. I mean like true Milestones! Help! Snort! Gnork! Berliner's in Indiana and I'm in Maryland, only I was just there five hours ago. I'm home coughing, snifflin' swallowin' laughing to myself, smiling, remembering.

But what? I'm not sure I know. Remembering people, places, things that were done, sounds, smells, feelings. That's what I'm remembering. Just walking, talking, crapping, sleeping, drinking, eating, thinking. U.S. 40. Heading west. Heading east. Brad, Roy, Tom, Steve. Chuck that snowball. Shit! I just missed him! What the hell should we do? Christ it's snowing. You want the bed or the floor? Oleo. Joshua. Goddam it get that cat outa here. Green Dolphin Street supplied the setting. Richmond in the rain. Feet are frozen. "Thanks for coming Jay." Smiling, happy, walking away, looking for a ride, get there right up to the airport, caught that TWA in fifteen minutes flat. Relaxin' in the warm cabin, stretching, moving' climbing, faster, ears are popping, sun is brilliant, clouds dissolve, covering miles without moving, resting and remembering. You're Berliner. I am Levy, in this world with a real friend, can't forget you cause you are you. Crazy old flannel shirts, chocolate chip cookies, cheese fondue, hot dogs with melted cheese, reading Dostoevsky, Kafka, writing, speaking thinking, breathing, planning. History of Art. Wish I knew. Nappy keep quiet. Your house on a cold snowy day in January. Fire sometimes going. Music playing. Phone might ring. Pick up Kathy. Come on downstairs. Listening to Miles, Monk. Sitting in your basement, smoking, talking, and thinking. Chickering or Steinway. Steinway wins eight out of nine. Sounding good, feeling good. Letting go. Moving out. Probably just a release. What is a music? Well here's a music I got in a jelly jar last summer out looking for fireflies. It just flew in and hummed and hummed.

Going away but coming back. Hup two three four. Let me hear you chicken ass bastards. Yeah but I'm coming back. And I'm going to learn and think and talk and drink and make love not to mention fuck and kiss. Sketches of young Peter Berliner in England. Kinda tweedy. Foggy day in London town. Had me low and had me down. Thinking of you. No real total, just feeling and desperately trying to think. Her eyes get grey and cloudy then the rain begins to fall. Pitter patter pitter patter. I get a kick outa chitlins. Kalamazoo and Earlham too. Go Quakers. Jesus you mean you can't smoke. Run for your life Brad. Hey is the window open. Large with pepperoni. Heartburned and happy. Shall we get a Powerhouse? Oh, that bad are they? Mary Quaker is a virgin. Life is 33.33333 over. Get movin'. Start talking. Why not mean something and especially for yourself. I know Peterberliner. I remember him when he was 19. Guess that's all. Saying so long, but only for a while. Goddamn it. I thought of you. Grinning again. Thanks.

Jay

The next thing I knew, I heard from Larry.

November 8, 1966 (letter from LH to PB)

Pete

Since I won't have the time for a week to sit down at my magic typewriter and compose some rather poetical gem of a letter, I'm taking the time now between serious study and class to write some sort of proof of my existence. At this very moment you may or may not care to know, I'm sitting here drinking a mud-like coffee and smoking a Winston. My mind is stuffed full with about 295 years of American history in preparation for a fucking *midterm exam tomorrow. I feel tired and headachish, sort of unbathed and generally black.*

Levy returned, happy to have seen you and basically resigned to his fate. I'd be really interested in your impressions of his visit, also was some talk of progress concerning your story (the one entitled Stanley, you bastard).

There are things happening to me that are causing changes in my outlook and philosophy. There are books that have been read and people that have influenced my development in a variety of ways. But I can't write it now I'm still in the process of discovering. When you return I will hopefully be ready to share all of this with you.

I've driven to Baltimore but Susie was at Pembroke. I've bought a car— a 1961 white Volvo 544. I've let my hair grow long. I've kissed Phyllis Duvall. I've been to Matt Kane's a lot. I've maintained about a B average although this week's mid semester exams will tell the tale.

Please write.

Larry

Classes were getting more demanding. We were sophomores and expected to step up our game. Philosophy was taught by a crusty professor with a Southern accent who looked a lot like Dave Brubeck. He took the subject very seriously but not without humor. I took notes furiously, promising myself I would research all the references he rat-tatted off. We were exploring the nature of courage. In my mind it was synonymous with nerve. As in, you have a lot of *nerve* or you just need to get up the *nerve*. Nerve was a good thing. Especially when you had to stand up to a bully, ask a girl on a date or bluff your way into a bar. But it had its limits. Jay had nerve. *Damn the consequences.* But too much is foolish. You can get by on it if you're lucky. But nobody's lucky all the time.

We read *Courage to Be* by Paul Tillich, who traced every concept to the original Greek. *Am I going to have to study Greek?* Aristotle said that to withstand pain and death courageously is *noble*—a virtue to which we should aspire. The greatest test of courage is self-sacrifice. No one epitomizes courage more than a soldier who stands ready to sacrifice his life.

I wondered if I was capable of courage. I thought of *Captain Courageous* and the *Red Badge of Courage*, and how Hemingway and Mailer and Salinger all went to war. Shouldn't I go as well, if only to test my courage? Plus there was no better place to write the Great American Novel than in the trenches.

Socrates had a different take. He equated courage with acting on the knowledge of what is good and evil. Thomas Aquinas said that courage is "strength of mind. United with wisdom. Capable of conquering whatever threatens the attainment of the highest good."

Isn't that the courage of Gandhi? Of Dr. King? Of pacifists, protesters, and war resisters?

November 12, 1966 (letter from PB to LH)

Larry,

Snow. And I, boot-clad and scarf-clad venture out into the foreboding drifts, and wet, stinging flurries, and like some Tolstoyan figure bearing a sack of grain, carry a week's worth of dirty clothes to the laundry, as timber wolves snarl hungrily in the parking lot.

I recently received a damn nice card from the mad and blonde Phyllis, and will write her back soon. I also received your amazing and trenchant letters.

The news here is that there was this terrifically inspiring concert by Phil Ochs (the long-haired, unwashed folk singer that he is) here in Goddard Hall (place of weekly convocations, concerts, and lectures). In the short time he was here, he managed to shock and irritate a hell of a lot of people. He is not one to pull punches and sang some amazing songs, which stirred up a lot of reaction on campus.

We have regular protests going on. They are painfully Quaker-like and polite, but they seem to serve a purpose. The marchers get both support and abuse. The old grub vs. jock opinion board rage is brought to a peak; the jocks scream sonofabitch at the grubs and the grubs quote Socrates, Thoreau and David Dubinsky.

There is something called Weekly Vigil for Peace in Vietnam every Wednesday at noon. It always strikes me as absurd. I mean, 30 or 40 people standing silently in the middle of a campus in the middle of nowhere while a war is raging on the other side of the earth. The snow is flying, and I find myself joining them--hood up, stamping my feet to stay warm—shivering for the next hour wondering what the hell we are doing. I can only answer for myself. The gist is this. We are here because this war that is very real and very present—even to those of us on this idyllic and secure campus. It is real enough to be a danger to my brother who is somewhere in Vietnam as we speak. Real enough that it threatens to annihilate his and other people's best efforts to build a better world. Real enough to make me wonder if I am supporting it simply by saying nothing.

So we are standing as a group—-not even expressing an opinion (taking a stand) or raising hell or screaming at the perpetrators. Just standing. Simply drawing attention in the middle of an ordinary day to what is going on far, far away, hoping people will reflect (even superficially) on what is going down.

I can't tell you how wild and great it was to see that curly-haired, piano-blowing, army-bound sonofabitch sitting in my room here in the bread-basket of the nation. The fantastic thing was that he (Levy, Jay M.) was goddam un-sad if not downright enthused about living, breathing, eating, drinking, the whole hang-up called Life and I do think there is a god—whether its Monk or Miles or Damon Runyan or whoever. Shit. Whew. And Hot Damn to see his face smiling even when he's leaving for six unlucky months: to hear him talk in his very distinctively Levy-dialect—to hear him talk like no one else in the world for three or four or six (Chagall-leaping) hours on a Steinway baby grand. But, you must know what I'm talking about.
Life is too fast-flowing if you ask me.
Pete

While the rest of us were dreading military service, Jay was living it. It still seemed unreal. But proof of it soon landed in my mailbox.

November 16, 1966 (letter from JL to PB)
Fort Jackson South Carolina
Dear Peter Berliner
*   A thousand Siddarthian pardons for not writing sooner but the Army affords little time for anything. So much has happened since I got here that*

it is truly impossible to relate the occurrences in any logical order. The Army is simply nothing but pure insanity plus general harassment. Except for the few guys I'm friends with who have some intelligence, the whole experience has been monotonous, dull and a total waste of time. When I get home for good, I'm going to devote all my spare time in convincing and preventing you, Larry and Bob from ever becoming affiliated with any military.

I miss your Berliner face and words as much as I miss the piano, Miles, Monk and Evans. God I hope I can still play the damn thing. Oh well only one more week till I get out of here on December 19th, and then I have two weeks of pure, beautiful unadulterated freedom.

I'll tell you one thing right now. Every damn thing that happened in Catch 22 has happened here. That book is no novel. I'll try to elaborate. First of all my entire company lives in tents. The damn tents are so unbelievably drafty and cold that everyone sleeps with their heads under the covers. There are these two little oil burning stoves at each end of the tent but they do very little to warm up the freezing G.I.s. My tent is full of morons except one guy. I try to spend as little time as possible in that tent. Christ, you could lose your mind listening to some of these idiots babble all the time. I shall convey one amusing happening which took place about a week ago. Monday we had our physical training test and I must say it was quite exhausting. I did manage to pass it barely. When we got to the company area, we had a little time before chow formation so I laid down on my bed all aching and sore. I really felt miserable. I was cold, dirty, snotty, lonely, horny, sore throat, coughing, stuffed up nose, fevery and rather crappy.

I just laid there moaning and shaking. The rest of the guys came in the tent but of course did not notice anything because everyone here looks that way. They went to dinner. I didn't and I was still moaning and quaking when they came back. They became slightly concerned. "Anything wrong? They asked. I couldn't answer. It just became comfortable to moan and shake so I continued to do so. Finally, I was carried to the orderly room. The sergeants scratched their heads and look puzzled. They called an ambulance and took me to the hospital. The doctors didn't know what was wrong either so they knocked me out with 100 ccs of something or other. Peace and quiet and rest at last. I spent three beautiful days sleeping and *taking it easy. It was really great not to mention a first class acting job. Of course I'm back on the usual army swill. Oh well.*

Everyone here exists on memories—memories of home, of girls, of food, of sanitation, and comfort. I'm certainly no different. I yearn for my beautiful woman and to see you, Larry and Bob, to eat real food again and to be warm. I remember that great trip I had to Richmond, Indiana to see you and of Carpenter Hall and of that great Steinway. Ah memories!

I will be home soon I guess and then back to school. Lord I can't wait to crack the books and think and think and think. I'm dying for knowledge more now than ever in my life and I believe I want to teach.

Please write whenever possible. Mail is my only link to the outside world. Write whenever you can please. Say hello to your roommates for me. Take care and read a good book for me.
Pvt. Jay M. Levy
Fort Jackson, S. C.

Through the fall, I found myself contemplating the war and what to do about it. Some Earlham graduates had enlisted. A handful went to jail. Others became conscientious objectors. Some headed toward the northern border. Prime Minister Trudeau said:

> *Those who make a conscientious judgment that they must not participate in this war have my complete sympathy, and indeed our political approach has been to give them access to Canada. Canada should be a refuge from militarism.*

More than 100,000 Americans took him up on his offer.

November 21, 1966 (from LH to PB)
Berliner,

Levy, as you well realize, is Levy. At times I feel like a new intern with a patient on the critical list. Our friendship blooms, we are both important to each other for reasons that we can never verbalize, each to each. There is a cute and rather informal little foursome made of Jay, Phyllis, Adrienne and Larry. No pairing up, no stickiness. Just a bunch of kids who call for each other to come out and play in the sun. In this realm, Levy has changed

from sad to happy, morose to exuberant, reflective, inward and grumpy to
eccentric, outgoing and giggly. What a change. Very startling.

Cooper is an interesting study. He's half insane half existential man
and half child. He thinks, he feels and I would rather be with him than
with many people. Bob is immersed in frat life and I'm saddened somewhat,
but everyone has his own bag.
When are you coming home?
Larry

During winter break, Larry and I did a few all-night shifts at the Post Office in the days leading up to Christmas. Our attention to sorting mail hour after hour was enhanced considerably by the tiny pills (referred to them as uppers) that Larry generously shared. Apparently better living through chemistry was truly possible.

January 11, 1967 (letter from LH to PB)

God! What a mass of confusion but nonetheless interesting confusion
my life is. There are stories, my friends, stories I have to tell. First,
registration at Towson State Teacher's College was nifty and frightening. I
arrived I.D. in hand, slacks neatly pressed, haircut, face washed, and
shaved, and an hour early. I walk around the campus. I read everything
posted on 37 different bulletin boards, I examine a model of the School of
the Applied Arts proposed additions. Most of all I sweat from my armpits
and reconsider the whole scene.

"Look, "I remark to myself, "My scene is secure at Montgomery Junior
College. I'm known and loved and I'm popular. My mom is within walking
distance, I don't have to worry about missing dinner. My toothpaste is
purchased for me! So why oh why would I want to enter into a whole new
scene. I mean here I'm nobody! Help!" But then I punch myself in the
mouth (mentally of course) and stiffen my upper lip, bravely attend my
interview, and register for classes.

My amazing adventures with women has reached an interesting point.
As I thought and pondered it (it being the situation with Phyllis and
myself), I decided that the best mode of behavior would be to not say
anything to her about New Year's Eve. Utter silence, right.

Now in the meantime guess who I met, gassed, charmed, thrilled, kissed, touched, spoke tenderly and entirely endeared myself to? Guess....guess....give up? Okay—none other but the beautiful and delectable Nancy W. Da dum! So this Nancy-Larry thing was born and has developed into a white-hot temperature in but four short days. Right about the 6th day Phyllis (a green bough) sits down at a table with me and says quietly,

"May I speak to you please?"

That's when we retire to a secluded closet where she proceeded to tearfully explain how crucial I was to her, how she thought about me constantly, and how it couldn't just end. I didn't even know what to say. Then-- one, two three--just like that, she'd gone back together with her high school boyfriend.

Susie called tonight and said her parents were tripping off to New York this weekend why don't I bring my mind and my body to Baltimore for a couple of days and nights of love and kisses.
Wow, I feel all written out now.
Larry

As Larry moved toward a higher calling at Towson State Teachers College, Jay was serving his country at an Army Reserves camp in Indiana. Somehow, in the midst of it, he managed to tear himself away for another visit me at Earlham. As Jay wrote to Larry:

February 12, 1967 (letter from JL to LH)
Ft. Benjamin

Larry, I decided it was definitely time to write you some sort of letter. I took off this weekend from Uncle Ben's rest home to see Peter. Needless to say I'm writing this thing from Berliner's room. I read your latest letter, and I'm glad to hear that you are somewhere somewhat settled at Towson I should be coming home this weekend and of course will come up to see you.

Things are generally stagnant here, but I shall be released soon. It looks as if summer school is out, because I will probably have to go to summer camp with my unit. Oh well. Maybe this fall I'll make it. I did have a pretty good time this weekend here at old Earlham. Pete and I were bombed out of our minds on a fifth of Jack Daniels Black Label. I also spent quite a few of the better hours of my life playing one the college's Steinway grands. By the way, please try and pick up this great new record by Horace Silver called Cape Verde—very pretty and bluesy. It features J.J. Johnson. I'm sure you will dig it very much.

Jesus Christ I hardly know what to talk about. Life is pretty boring and after a while numb. At least Pete is giving me some literature to bring back with me that should ease the pain somewhat.

Have you heard from B.O.? Lord knows I haven't.

She-eet man set me up for a trip or something when I get home next week. Bennies, Dex, Big H—anything. My mind definitely needs an enema. I have been upset since I found out that Elvin Jones and Tony Williams are in jail in Tokyo Japan on trumped up drug charges. Christ when will they leave artists alone.

Let's all go to California this summer and pick grapes or something. I don't give a god damn. Or let's cut down some giant redwoods in Oregon or anything we haven't done before. Write me a good Horwitz letter or something immediately. I need help. Hey are we still friends? Goddammit Larry. I've got the worst feeling that you have forgotten me.

Help!! I'm a mushroom. Well You Needn't. Joshua. Walkin'. All Blues.

Actually, I'm going to devote my life to becoming a towel rack.

I'm sorry this is such a shitty letter. I guess I'm just in one of those stupid moods. I'll recover. Write if you get a chance. If not I'll see you this weekend regardless. The eagle flies on Friday. Saturday I go out to play.

Oh well take care and eat your prunes and keep the hairs in your nose clipped close.

J.M. Levy the third

I sent Larry my account of Jay's visit.

February 17, 1967 (letter from PB to LH)

Larry,

Somnolently; hazy; floating. Turned in a history paper just an hour ago after having worked on it all night. Enjoying that feeling of catharsis, I listen to Professor Steeples' passionate and moving explanation of how slavery was the cause of the Civil War, to the horror of all the students who had based their theses on economics as its primary motivation.

By the end of the class I felt beyond tired. The sidewalk is springy under my feet. What I feel like doing is cracking a beer, tripping up to Bob Ochsman's farm, and stopping to eat at Bell's. I'd like to be dropping over to where you are and have a cigarette, a quart bottle of Miller's within reach, and shooting the crap. Instead I'm gonna tell you about Levy's latest visit to my humble abode.

I could begin by discussing how the holy and anointed Jay has undoubtedly beat the system and that the chances are damn good that he'll be home before I will. Or I could start by explaining how there was this girl in my room at 4 a.m. Sunday morning, in violation of all the rules that Earlham holds so dear.

The first time Levy visited, we ended up polishing off immense amounts of alcohol in my room (a major violation worthy of immediate expulsion. On this visit we harbored an overnight guest of the female persuasion (cardinal rule number #2). Now I fear if he ever returns we will have run out of the obvious transgressions and have to resort to major felonies---serious narcotics, sodomy or assassination.

We spent the first couple of hours talking his adventures at Fort Benjamin Harrison—you know-- stuff about dorm life, the excellent food, the free afternoons and evenings. Lots of insanity abounds there but nothing like the shit he went through at Fort Jackson. He also spent a fair amount of time playing the piano, like the last time he was here.

Not having a car, and seeing as how the place was half-empty because of mid-term break, there wasn't a hell of a lot to do. There we were on a Saturday night with no place to go. It's bitterly cold outside and the forecast was for snow. Levy has a cold and his nose is flowing like a faucet. I am depressed by our lack of mobility.

Finally Levy, in an exasperated but cheerful way, says:

"Well Berliner, what (he pauses) would you be doing if Horwitz was here instead of me?"

"We'd probably run out and get a fifth, then go out to the graveyard to drink it."

"Okay," he says. "Let's do it."

We head out into the wintry blasts. We're shivering like crazy. We run into Roger Ide and persuade him to host this planned debauchery in his off-campus pad (warmer by far than the graveyard). By midnight, we are happily boozed, warm and comfortable. Riley, Lucy and Baily, among others, have joined us. Levy (our proud soldier) has assimilated neatly into this folk-ethnic crowd, and after putting on a stack of Brubeck records on the stereo, is contentedly talking happy shit to all who will listen.

At about 3:30 a.m. Levy and I and this freshman named Fran are stepping out onto the cold quiet, snow-crusted street on our way back to campus. Levy is striking up tunes from the Wizard of Oz on his melodica, and the three of us are high stepping merrily down the street. All the doors to her dorm are locked. Levy, being the gentleman, starts throwing chunks of snow and gravel against various dorm windows in hopes of finding someone who will open the door. This went on for quite a while to no avail.

Then Levy says: "Well gosh Fran, we could all go up to Pete's room—his roommates are gone. I mean after all."

"Jay," Fran says. "Yeah, but if we get caught, not only would I get kicked out, but Pete would too."

"Don't be ridiculous," was Jay's response.

She settled into Brad's bunk about ten minutes later. We all fell dead asleep. I woke to see her putting on my boots and overcoat and tear-ass down the stairs. I turned over and slept until one.

Words of importance: get ahold of John Barth's Floating Opera immediately. It will knock you on your sordid little ass. More to tell but running out of time.

Write soon. (Freak freely). Fly.

Pete

Chapter 9

Turn on. Tune Out.

Earlham was an island of progressive ideas in a conservative sea. Still, it was not immune from the currents of change. Although anything that was new or really mattered got its start on one of the coasts, it eventually got to Indiana.

Drug use was sweeping the country. Marijuana was rampant on campuses, and LSD, thanks to Dr. Timothy Leary, was becoming a drug of choice. Leary was at Harvard conducting experiments with LSD on prisoners. Then he started taking more trips than his subjects and sharing his mind-bending experiences with the world.

When it became public, Harvard warned its students about the perils of mind-altering drugs. The story went national, and it was *Reefer Madness* all over again. The New Jersey Drug Study Commission announced that LSD was "the greatest threat facing the country today—more dangerous than the Vietnam War." All the hyperbole about the dangers of drugs only fueled their spread. You could join the rebellion simply by buying or ingesting illicit substances.

LSD was supposedly about more than just getting high. People on LSD claimed to see God. LSD made them expand their consciousness, transcend their ego (whatever that meant) and change their heads (again, whatever that meant). For some, an LSD experience was an impetus to reimagine whatever path they were on or to decide to do nothing at all. Don't *Do.* Just *Be.* If a hundred people decided to join together to do nothing at all, it was called a *Be In. Turn on, tune in and drop out* became a mantra. Just by repeating it, you could horrify your parents, all your elders and the Establishment all in one fell swoop.

There was more. *New jargon! New fashions! Accessories!* Grow out your hair. Burn incense. Make a necklace out of cloves. Wear strange hats and outrageous clothes. And, to the horror of your relatives, answer only to the name *Sunshine*, *Morning Glory* or *Star Child*. The possibilities were endless.

March 4, 1967 (letter from LH to PB)

Pete

Yes yes yes. John Barth is good'n'bad. I read both the End of the Road and The Floating Opera.

Levy came to see me the weekend after he visited you. Somehow just seeing him and hearing him talk and being with him was more than normally meaningful to me. Lorraine came up with him, and they sort of forced me to call Susie (I had severed relations with her) so that the four of us could double - date "just like old times." We saw Blow Up which is a really great film and one you should see as soon as possible.

I was overcome inexplicably with loneliness for my family last weekend. I drove back to my house for a surprise visit. What happened was rather shocking and, in the vernacular, really turned my head around. It seems as though my parents had planned a little party for that night. Four couples were there for drinks and talking and coffee and cake. I stuck around not wanting to do anything but be with my family for a day and not wanting to see friends or go out with old flames.

At any rate I managed to devour about half of my father's fifth of Haig and Haig, and the whole assemblage got into a middle-class suburbanite conversation concerning LSD and the type of people involved with the drug. Naturally they were making these completely inaccurate statements which I gently corrected. It was really a pretty lively little discussion, me against the whole bunch of them, when my father says something like, "Well, Larry has always said that he'd give anything a try if he got the chance just so he could learn about it."

This for some reason causes a silence to fall, in a very pregnant way of course. Immediately my father looks me in the eye and says: "Isn't that right Lar?"

I shake my head affirmatively. Then he says: "Well have you ever tried it?" And I, very Gary Cooper like, said, "Yep."

I watched as my poor mother's face contorts and the entire room rocks with shock. I am somehow now in the position of defending the entire American drug situation from San Francisco to Takoma Park. My parents are really cool, however, and gave me no static (except my mother who castigated both my father and me for a horrendous lack of tact and discretion). They even seemed to stand behind me as I answered their friends' accusations. Christ!

I feel strangely content lately. I'm happy with whatever that means and to glide along with no bumps, which is potentially dangerous. I just learned that it will be nothing short of a miracle if I'm able to graduate in June. However I trust that our cross country trip is still a reality. When will you be home? When do you leave for London?

Write.

Larry

Jay's stint in the Army Reserves did not last. He managed to power through boot camp and go on to special training at a post office. He attended several weekend training camps. But the Army, he decided, was not for him. So he packed up his equipment and gave it to the sergeant. "I'm quitting," he explained.

"The fuck you are Private. You cannot quit the Reserves."

"But I am," Jay said and walked away, keeping his Army jacket.

As he soon learned, you cannot quit the Army. He soon received an order to go to another physical as a prelude to re-induction. Before going, however, Jay visited Dr. Rosenberg, a psychiatrist, at his office in Chevy Chase. Prior to the visit, Jay ingested half a tab of acid. The office walls began to undulate as the session began. After an hour, most of which Jay spent playing the doctor's baby grand, he emerged with an official letter attesting to his mental instability.

Thus armed, Jay waited for the army bus on the corner of Eastern and Georgia Avenue, mentally preparing for what everyone had to go through. Lining up. Stripping. Hearing a voice behind you order: *Drop your briefs.* Waiting for your turn to bend over, spread your cheeks, and practically choke as some beefy guy with a rubber glove pokes his finger up your rectum. As you wait you wonder: *Do people actually volunteer for this duty? Do they ever find what they are looking for? Exactly how many assholes are probed before they put on a new glove?* You squirm some more. When that's done, you go piss into a cup.

While waiting for the bus to arrive, someone suggested that Jay choke down some chocolate bars before getting on board. He went across the street to Hofberg's Deli and bought eight Milky Ways. Later that day, after his urine was tested, an officer told him with great concern, "I'm sorry son. We're not going to able to take you. You are in an advanced state of diabetes. I suggest you get immediate medical attention."

I came home for spring break and packed up for my semester abroad. I was going to study in London for three months in London with my English professor, Paul Lacey, his wife Margaret, and 12 other Earlham students. I planned to spend the summer hitching around Europe. In a week I would go to New York to set sail on the *S.S. United States*.

Before I left, Cooper bestowed me a tab of acid and offered to guide my first LSD trip. I knew I was getting high when I found myself seriously engrossed in the colorful patterns in an oily puddle outside Cooper's house. I spent quite a while watching it evolve into glowing, animated works of modern art. This prompted us to drive to the Phillips Gallery where I observed great works of art dissolve into mud puddles. As we were driving home, Larry asked if everything was crispy clear. "I don't know," I said. "What did it look like before?" I spent the last stages of the trip at home, listening to Miles Davis on our stereo, trying not to say a word to anyone.

Two days later, I set sail for England. After a couple of days of rain and rough seas, I sought sunlight on uppermost deck. It was windy, chilly and damp, but glimmering shafts of sunlight broke through the clouds and glanced on the surface of the sea. The sun brought out even those who had been confined in their cabins, head throbbing, stomach churning, cursing the roll of the ocean. It began to warm, and we whiled away the day playing shuffleboard or leaning against the railings, mesmerized by the patterns of spray and foam colliding against the ship's steel hull. We indulged in the ship's bountiful buffets of Waldorf salad, roast beef, turkey and duck, oxtail soup, shrimp cocktails, green turtle soup, lobster bisque, and pate de foie. We also took advantage of the 24-hour room service, once ordering sandwiches, ice cream and cookies for eight of us at four in the morning. This continued another three days until we debarked at Southampton and boarded the train to London.

April 16, 1967 (letter from PB to LH)

Dear Larry,

I am living in Finsbury Park, four miles from the centre of London in a three story row-house, with the proprietors, Mr. and Mrs. Bull, Rick, my roommate from Earlham, and Rich, the boarder on the floor above, who says the housing around here is London's worst. Judging from the varying degrees of dilapidation, broken windows and crowded lots, he may be right. Yet the people in our neighborhood are friendly and warm. It is generally very quiet until around 11 o'clock when the pubs close. Even then the noise only lasts a little while. We are outside London proper but it's easy to get around on buses and on the tube.

From my bedroom I can see long rows of houses with discolored brick walls and sharply slanted roofs in need of repair. At night, the rows of chimneys, crooked and black, loom like evil spirits against the dark sky. When it rains everything turns gray—the pavement, the houses, the sky. The air is dense with city smells—exhaust, trash, rotting flowers and discarded fruit. When the sun comes out, it is hot and still humid, and the subways are hellish. But I love living in the city. If I consult the subway maps and arm myself with my copy of A to Zed, I can go anywhere.

There are at least six pubs within two blocks of us. Mr. Bull tells Eric (my roommate from Earlham) and me to avoid the Earl of Essex because there are "nothing but Irish and darkies there."

"Go to the Bricklayers," he says. "It doesn't have a telly and jukebox and radio all going at the same time, and is a good place for a couple of blokes to have a quiet chitchat."

So Rick and I head to the Earl of Essex. We go through the entrance to the Saloon. Although they serve liquor, everyone is drinking ale or Guinness. The women are drinking Shandys, a mix of lager and lemonade. We order a pint of bitter which is on tap and only costs three bob (about 50 cents.) The beer is warm and strong. That's how they like it. If you ask for a bottle, they take the bottle from right off a shelf. Cold beer is looked down upon and asking for ice in a drink is blasphemous. But it's good, when you get used to it and three or four will knock you on your ass.

Then we go out of the Saloon and through the other entrance into Pub side. That's where the Irish and the other common folks go. It's smokier and the air is stale. There are men playing darts and betting. On Sunday nights, we're told, there are sing-songs.
Enough for now.
Pete

We went to classes, museums, and plays. We wandered the city. I was thrilled to be in the haunts of so many writers, philosophers, artists and kings, and to experience the palpable weight of history and time. The food was disappointing. We couldn't find a hamburger that measured up even to McDonalds. We ate fish and chips wrapped up in greasy newsprint and sausages served with spicy hot mustard sold from sidewalk stands. At the Bull's we dined on overdone roast beef, roast potatoes, bangers and mash, and steak and kidney pie. We even tried haggis.

In the evenings, Rick and I went to a pub or ventured to Soho and Carnaby Street to absorb the latest music, fashion, and art. One night, I went off on my own. I took the subway from Finsbury Park to Russell Square. I walked past Harrods, Marks and Spencer, offices, banks, posh restaurants, pubs (the *Duke of Wellington,* the *Squire, Fox & Anchor,* the *Rising Sun*), and cinemas. Then I chanced upon a rail-thin man with washed-out eyes and stringy red hair. He wore an orange, red and purple silk scarf and was nailing psychedelic posters that advertised *UFO Tonight and Every Night 43 Tot. Ct. 10:30 to dawn.* I was intrigued.

"Where exactly is this place?" I asked.

"Down the street," he pointed, "At the Blarney Stone. But it's only the Blarney Stone until half past ten."

It was still early, so I went into a pub for a pint, then walked to where there was crowd of people wearing granny glasses and colorful mod clothing, colorful, improbable and bold. Some were holding flowers or incense.

Three young women came over. One asked the red-haired poster boy how much to get in. "25 bob for membership, and 10 more to get in." (About $5).

"Will there be dancing?" Yes, he said.

"Is there a floor show?"

"Indeed," he said, "and several continental movies, jazz, strobe, a bit of everything."

"Sounds delightful," she said, but her friend said, "It's probably not worth it for only an hour."

"You can stay 'til dawn if you like," said the poster man, but the girls just giggled and said perhaps another time.

The last train left at midnight so I had to decide whether to go home then or stay all night. When the doors opened, I found a member to take me in. Descending from the stately streets of London, the epicenter of civility, into the chaos below was crossing the great cultural divide. I was confident that my parents would have hated everything about it.

The hall was lined with mirrors. Music blared in a hellish cacophony as though all works of Bach were playing at the same time. Strange black and white images were projected onto sheets hanging from rafters. Spinning spotlights beamed protoplasmic patterns onto the walls. The music shifted at ear-splitting intensity from choruses of calliopes to Wagnerian shouting matches. The hall was filling rapidly with young men dressed like peacocks, with long flowing locks and facial hair that made Blackbeard look like an Army recruit. The girls (birds) wore mini-skirts that exposed delectably pale thighs and asses. It was a sight to see. In time, the music gave way to acid rock (*Jefferson Airplane, Jimi Hendrix, Cream*) as fumes from burning grass and hashish wafted in the air.

I wandered like a lost lamb amid the sweaty mass of flesh. I was alternately intrigued, shocked, appalled. I was a stranger in a foreign land literally and metaphorically. I tried to embrace the madness, lose myself in the music, and groove to all sensual delights. I fixated on the floating patterns of light that flowed like colonies of neon flagella.

I had to ask. "How do you make that happen?"

"Warmth," said the goggle-eyed hippie behind the projector, "and by injecting different chemicals onto the slides."

The soundtrack was paused for an announcement:

Happening 44 is on for tomorrow night. Film. Strobes. Sounds. There will be a picnic at the bandstand at Kensington Gardens on Sunday. There will be food (cheers) provided by two of our friends here. Everyone is invited to come, eat, turn on, and make love.

A film came on at midnight. The dancers flopped on the floor. Images raced over them. Wheat fields waving. Tall buildings breathing. Animal carcasses, intestines, bleeding entrails, and pigs being slaughtered. Close ups - octopi, eels and jellyfish. Undulating rocks, sand dunes and skulls. *Are they alive? Are we dead? Is it almost over?* The music switched to John Cage electronic music—dissonant and hard. A slaughterhouse. A butcher shop. A meat slicer in a deli. Female bodies. Backs arched. Orgasmic smiles. Enormous breasts that filled the screen. Gigantic nipples, noses, toes, arms and thighs. Pubic hair waving in the wind. An image of a penis filled the screen. The camera pulled back. A naked man dancing. Commuters crowding sidewalks. Fade to black. Credits. A final frame: *Thanks to a grant from the Ford Foundation.*

By then, the air was heavy with sweat and smoke. It was hard to breathe. I walked up the stairs and gulped in the moist, fresh air. The streets were empty but for the black taxis that sped by like night scavengers. I walked toward the city center. Two West Indians stopped to ask the time. I looked blearily at my watch, and told them it was half past three. One of them guessed that I was Canadian. I told them I was. They decided to wait for a bus. I left them there.

The city was cast in a silence that was interrupted in turn by a group of people standing outside a long-closed Spanish restaurant, a well-dressed man sobbing on the stoop in front of a hat shop, and a drunk stumbling down the sidewalk and spitting at anyone who came close. I walked down Tottenham Court Road toward Trafalgar Square, stopping for a hot cuppa in an all-night café. I came upon Covent Garden where heavily loaded lorries were crowding the streets. I could hear brakes screeching, gears rasping, tailgates clanging, and the thunderclaps of crates of produce being dropped in alleys. The clattering of the trucks unloading continued to crescendo as workmen wheeled stacks of crates to the stalls inside.

I continued my weary wander along Bow St. The air swelled with the earthy smells of cabbage, potatoes, carrots, and turnips; the sweet scent of Israeli oranges, grapefruit, and lemons, and the delirious odors of fresh cut chrysanthemums, daffodils, lilac and roses trucked from Salisbury. As the sun began to rise, I walked ecstatically through the market, not quite believing where I was nor understanding how I got there.

April 25, 1967 (letter from LH to PB)

Pete

Your letter received, happily and read repeatedly by me in an effort, I suppose, to inhale somehow the essence of this experience which we, sadly, are not sharing. I love thinking about the things you see and touch and smell every day. Things that are apparently insignificant which become in the end, the most crucial things. Things which you are hopefully recording and remembering and saving to share with us when summer finally ends. There are many tales and joyful noises that I have to tell you, but somehow they pale when I look at the address to which I am sending this epistle.

Levy has turned into a hippie. He and Cooper spend hours concocting all manner of hysterical and fantastic plans. Me, sick and down in Silver Spring, then Florida, then Baltimore and in Silver Spring again. My ailment was finally diagnosed as the dreaded mononucleosis. Then, in response to the danger of my missing the entire semester, I chose to ignore the disease, and experienced all the bad changes that went along with that.

A scene for your enjoyment. Larry is asleep and deathly in the health center on the charming campus of Towson State. The time is 6:30 a.m. The same Larry is awakened by a series of explosions which turned out to be Cooper slamming his fists against my huge window. I look out through the blinds to see Levy dressed in blue denim jeans, a denim jacket and GI combat boots, and Tommy Howell dressed in a flowing George Washington-style coat, a powdered wig and steel rimmed grannie glasses, and Cooper wearing a psychedelic necktie and a weird suede jacket.

"Quick," cries Cooper hysterically, "Get into some clothes and get out through the window. We're going to New York and you have to come." I am struck speechless. Levy lifts this huge boot over the window sill, nearly splitting his body in the effort, and says, "Tell me you like my shoes Horwitz. Go on and tell me you really like them. It'll make my whole day."

Howell is giggling like a demented person at everything. I mumble excuses and apologies as Levy tells me to hurry as a campus policeman examines his still-running car which contains a sleeping girl, Cooper's latest piece. Suddenly the three of them break into an impromptu ballet with Levy and Cooper doing impossible pas de deux. They dance their way into the car and leave me, sad and lonely and sick, but also happy from their wild and inexplicable visit.

Other scenes.

Levy, a beautiful poet on LSD, weeping over the beauty of tulips, weeping over the fact that you are far away, and presiding over a dinner of submarine sandwiches.

Susie and myself together again. I'm teaching her how to smoke pot. She has been accepted at Antioch, University of Chicago, Barnard and Brandeis. I am humbled before her. She is no longer the girl we shocked by saying curse words while we tried to grow up. She now purchases her own special contraceptive equipment before we see each other.

I am constantly saddened by death.

Larry

Our studies in England were light. We had plenty of time to spend in pubs and explore. One evening, we gathered at *The*

Lion and the Tortoise, a pub nearby the University of London. The discussion got around quickly to the war. Our professor and tour guide Paul Lacey was with us. In addition to teaching he was also on the board of the American Friends Service Committee. Over pints of Guinness Stout, I asked when he first knew he was a pacifist.

"I was raised a Quaker. Pacifism is something that is at the core of my faith. It wasn't so much that I chose to be a pacifist as much as I never thought of myself as anything but one."

"But do you ever have doubts? "

"Sure. Like any belief, it's always being tested. And no one is immune to feelings of aggression or even vengeance. But whenever that arises, I reflect on some essential truths."

"Such as?"

'That God is within us, that we are guided by an inner light, and that we are responsible for acting in accordance with that guidance.

"Are all Quakers pacifists?"

"By no means, but it is a part of its tradition. As far back as 1661, Quaker leaders renounced the use of weapons and war. Not far from where we are sitting, as a matter of fact. It was during a rather bloody civil war and a time when Quakers were being persecuted. George Fox presented to Charles the Second a treatise called: *A Declaration from the Harmless and Innocent People of God called Quakers against All the Plotters and Fighters of the World.*"

"There's a title if I ever heard one."

"It is a mouthful."

"Being a pacifist," Paul went on, "is not without challenges. You can be jailed for refusing induction, for one. And you have to find non-violent ways to resolve conflict and fight for justice. Pacifism doesn't mean passivity."

"But that's a discussion worthy of another pint," he concluded, and I agreed.

May 2, 1967 (letter from PB to LH)

London

Last Friday, our merry group of scholars took off in a motor coach (as they say here) to Canterbury. The cathedral there is a massive stone edifice. Inside, it is crowded with English school girls who are furiously taking notes, and tourists—American and otherwise—armed with Kodak Instamatics. From there we went to Dover. Above the town is Dover Castle which was built in the 12th century to fend off the French. We hopped off the bus like school kids and tore up the hill to explore tunnels and underground rooms with openings just wide enough for a crossbow or two. We can see the famous white cliffs. Matthew Arnold's poem comes to mind, "the sea is calm tonight / the moon lies fair upon the straights." I stare out at the water hoping to glimpse the French coast, but see only the water and a few large ships easing their way into the harbor.

It is four o'clock. Time to get on the coach to go back to London. But the sun is still shining and it's too nice to go back. Without a lot of forethought, Barb Mills (a junior art major) and I grab our knapsacks, step off the bus and wave goodbye.

"I'd like a cigarette," Barb says,

"But you don't smoke."

"Yes, but right now I feel like a cigarette," she says.

"Here's one, love," I say comfortingly, using my best British inflection.

We smoke and search out the youth hostel. We eat spaghetti at a tiny café. Then we walk down to the sea, on a beach of water-smoothed pebbles—a fantastic place to run and dance and listen to the sounds we make. We follow the shoreline until we find a path leading up the hillside. We sprawl on the coarse grass at the top of the hill as the sun sinks below the fortress. We gaze at the misty sea and the outline of the castle against the dimly lit sky, then amble back down through tangled grass and wildflowers. In the glow of the red-sky, Barb is natural and youthful and the perfect person to walk with in a far land. I am hopelessly in love.

The next day, we hitchhike along the southern coast to the town of Rye where Henry James wrote Turn of the Screw. We get a ride from two Pakistani to Hastings by the Sea, and stay the night at another hostel. From there, we get a long ride in a Range Rover. The driver is about 30, nice looking, with long, carefully coifed hair. He is wearing a pink shirt and a tie and sunglasses. Barb gets in the front seat. I get in the back.

"Are you from here?" Barb asks

"Well now, I don't suppose anyone's really from here. They just live here. I actually live in Brighton, which is west of London. You should go sometime."

He asks where we are from. "Washington D.C. and Michigan," Barb answers, "If that means anything. Have you been to the states?"

"Only to New York. Four times. Smashing place. Wonderful city. So alive," he says.

We are winding our way through sheep country. The sheep are heavy with wool. It's hard to go fast because the roads seem to go in circles. He explains that his work takes him to New York, adding that he is a fashion director.

"I used to go there when it was the fashion center. But no longer. America's become way too conservative these days." He runs four Snob Shops. "Boutiques we call them for want of a better word. Have you seen them? Very chic. Colorful. Music playing. A place for all the bloody vegetables to meet their friends on Saturday."

"Vegetables?"

"Absolutely. Maybe I'm being harsh, but I'm not far wrong. The English girl wouldn't spend her money on a book or see a play. She spends it on clothes or makeup. She doesn't know any better. We change the fashion so she won't get bored, and because she will buy anything. The purples and violets and greens that you see are part of a short trend. We're coming out with an entire new spring line. It's all part of Swinging England, you know," he says. "It's the most important thing they believe in. It keeps me in business."

"What about when they are older?" Barb asks.

"Vegetables."

"And they have the pubs?"

"To be vegetables in. The British are lethargic. They don't bother working very hard. Taxes take up too much of what they earn anyway, so they see no use in climbing to a higher bracket. Everything is much too traditional. Now there is the Common Market. If we don't get in now, we're *rather washed out as a nation. Well, it's washed out now, I suppose. But then it really would be washed out."*

He takes us to Chatham on the Thames and points us toward the road to London. We stop for cheese rolls and tea. We make our way through the town and, fantastically, past one of the Snob Shops. There's music, and the place is crowded with birds.

"You are all vegetables!" we scream. But nobody is listening.

The last ride was best. We covered 30 miles in two hours in an overloaded lorry—two hours filled with tales from an Irish truck driver, nine years out of the British secret service. He tells us about Gypsies and road prostitutes, and about growing up in a valley in the "oulde sod," where his world consisted of six families surrounded by hills, and everyone spoke Gaelic. I must go there soon.

He drops us off near Trafalgar Square in time to see men and women in costume dancing under the monument to Lord Nelson.
More to come,
Pete

June 7, 1967 (letter from PB to LH)

Dear Larry,

I was happy to hear from you. After reading your letter about 3,700 times, it was starting to get sort of boring. I can't make this very long because I have a lot of packing to do before I leave London on Friday to go to Paris. I will be there until Sunday then go on to a work camp in Evreux for a week or two. I don't know how the hell I'm going to speak French, but I guess I'll try.

You neglected to give me Ochsman's address. If you go away, I will send a letter through Jay. Is he still with us?

Going to Israel is a tremendous idea. There has been a large group of Israeli students and British Jews talking about going for the same purpose. There was also a demonstration in Hyde Park with about 10,000 people wearing blue shirts and blue arm bands and speaking in Yiddish accents. Twelve people were arrested at Speakers Corner after a Palestinian guy initiated a Long Live Nasser chant. The last I heard, the State Department wasn't allowing Americans to go to Israel. I don't feel sorry for Israel in any case. It seems to be smashing the Arabs to smithereens. At this rate, the war *should last only a month. It's not surprising to hear about support in America. It's very apparent here as well. If you do go, best of luck and write at length. I can pick up my mail in Paris at the end of June: C/O American Express, 101 Champs Elysees Paris, France.*

Bon Chance

Pete

June 21, 1967 (letter from LH to PB)

Pete,

Just to bring you up to snatch, Levy and Cooper and Snyder are now living in this fantastic apartment in Takoma Park. The apartment is really the entire top floor of one of those real old and stylish houses that one finds in Takoma Park. They live two blocks away from another pretty cool apartment which houses Phyllis Duvall and about six other chicks who shall remain nameless. Next door to Phyllis lives the infamous Michelle, and I won't dwell on that. The trio's apartment has three big bedrooms. There is a large bathroom located in the middle of the house which prevents free passage to pedestrian traffic when anyone is shitting.

There is a big old kitchen and a living room filled with low couches and a thousand dollars' worth of sound equipment, and a lot of cool things to look at and play with, and there are a lot of candles. It has been designated the "head room." I suppose I could go on and on about the scene here but the whole subject is frightfully boring.

I'm just afraid you will come back and not understand what has happened to us. Let me say that the pot/acid thing has become a natural accepted part of what's happening in our lives. I'm sorry we turned Levy on because he abuses and misuses and depends on the drugs. Cooper and I have discussed the whole thing at length and concluded nothing. It's just a part of our little game of life and we go ahead and groove with it. I try and not let it get out of control or to take up too much of my time, but it does.

Your dog was just here at my parent's house. He urinated in the damn bushes and walked into my house and schlepped around looking for, I swear, his beloved master. He walks pretty slow and stiffly, and his face is almost all this ash white color. Your sister will graduate from Sidwell in a few days and I will be there, I suppose, in your stead.

Of course the news of the week is that I will be going to Israel next week. My passport will arrive at my house in three days, I am getting several vaccinations on Monday and I will be going there to work so that some Israeli can go to the front to help prevent the raving hoards from engulfing the Jewish state.

I'm sure you are pretty aware of the reaction to the Acaba situation but it's really frantic around these parts. The American Jew can be pretty damn annoying at times but there is no end to their spirit and desire to help in situations like this. My mother is forever running to rallies and meetings not to mention writing, every day, to senators and congressmen. The local congregations have collected more than 750,000 dollars and contributions in about 10 days. The most un-Jewish Jews and the most un-Zionist Zionists are working and contributing and trying to help in any way. I don't have to explain my position to you. You are knowledgeable enough about my feelings towards Zionism and Israel.

I'm excited and a little nervous. You can expect that we will trade notebooks when we finally meet again and talk for weeks about the things that we have learned and discovered. Needless to say I hope you have an enjoyable summer, will I be able to send and receive letters from you later? Goodbye again. I will speak to you in September.
Larry

I was standing outside the *Old Vic Theater* in the heart of London, waiting for the play to begin. Barb and I were shooting the breeze.

"I'm kind of worried about what's going on back home," she confessed.

"What are you worried about?"

"Well, you know I've been going out with Eric for the last couple of quarters. But I got this letter from Peggy and she said that he's spending a lot of time with this freshman girl. I don't even know who she is."

"What's her name?"

"Lucy Dougall."

"Oh. I know her. She's kind of cool. But I don't think you should worry about her," I said.

At the time, I was nursing a major crush on Barb so it didn't occur to me that someone might choose Lucy over her. But it did get me thinking.

The first time I met Lucy was a few months before I set sail for England. She was a freshman in the class behind me. Lucy was hard to miss. She was five foot two, with blue eyes, and long, untamed flaxen hair. Though small in stature, she had a large presence and a great laugh. You knew it the minute she came into the room. She seemed to disregard all the things you are supposed to do or wear or say. She tooled around campus on a used green bicycle, wearing an Eskimo parka and a black Chilean hat.

That winter, she found her way into a group of people I sometimes hung out with. They were mostly what we called grubs or beats or hippies. They included Connie Hay and Riley, Amy Joy and a bunch of others whose tastes tended toward folk music, political protest and sandals. They were more likely to show up at the Guarded Well By coffee house than the Green Dolphin. They rode bikes and wore long scarves, and listened to Phil Ochs, Tom Paxton and Bob Dylan. Brad and Roy liked Lucy as well. She had a way of talking that amused them endlessly. I remember in particular her telling us a story about some guy when Brad said, "Tell me again who you are talking about." "You know," she answered. "The cat who split with the chick."

I was attracted by her energy and style. She was very hip-looking and lovely in a way that snuck up on me until I was seeing her and no one else.

Our term in London ended in June. Like other students, I planned to spend the summer traveling in Europe. Some were going off together. I resisted the urge to pair up and took off on my own. After taking the bus to the far reaches of London, I found my way to the road to Dover and started to hitchhike. I wondered if I would meet anyone along the way.

June 27, 1967 (letter from LH to PB)

Pete,

One of the things that made me move out of the apartment in Takoma Park which Cooper, Levy, Snyder and I shared was that I was witness to the collapse of all communication between Ochsman and Levy.

Bob came home from school and was perplexed by the drug-filled world in which we were living. He was completely dismayed by Jay's LSD-driven personality changes. Almost all of our talk and actions were mystifying to Bob, and I was suddenly struck by the possibility that the same horrible sad and abrupt barrier could exist between you and me.

Another major cause of my sudden reversal (complete with total confessions to my fine parents and rejection of all previous activities) was the amazingly difficult and complex mental hell hole I was constantly experiencing. I cannot reconcile 19 years of standard ethics and morality with less than a year of new morality and freedom from American Puritanism. In a word I kept thinking of my mother every time I lit up a ted.

I will try to convey the scene in that apartment. No one worked. There is never any food in the larder. Music (Beatles, Jefferson Airplane and other such) played constantly and each day was spent scoring and utilizing drugs. We smoked tea and hash to such an extent that the place was saturated with their sweet smell. DMT and LSD were used with less frequency but often enough so that their use was not considered unusual.

The pattern was basic and unchanging. The culmination was reached last Saturday with Cooper and Levy (hours after his return from army summer camp) and I ingesting 200 micrograms of acid at about 2 o'clock in the afternoon, and then in the course of the evening, used DMT and marijuana, I suddenly began (in Cooper's words) speaking "aggressively" and managed to severely criticize everyone. As more people arrived, more drugs were used. I can't even describe the real flavor of psychosis that was rampant.

I just finally quit, went home, took a tranquilizer and talked to Bob for several hours and to my parents for many more. They were sympathetic and not mad and happy to see me back home. I feel empty, sad, slightly confused and unsure of almost everything, but I'm straight now and I swear I'll be straight till I see you.

I read your half French/half English letters and how I wish I were with you, digging it. The war in Israel was over and done with so quickly and so successfully that I blinked and missed my chance to have an experience of great value. Oh well. I've discovered how hard everything sometimes is, and I've got a minor infection, similar to gonorrhea.
Larry

July 6, 1967 (letter from PB to LH)

Evreux, France
Larry,

Thank you for your letter. It was happy and sad. I've read it over many times—perhaps in search for the words with which to respond. It was strange to come home at Christmas to find a scene that was so switched around that I didn't really feel a part of it. I guess I had some of the same feelings as Bob. Not that I feel distant from you and Jay, but a lot of those scenes made me sad. I've been thinking back on my acid trip that Sunday before I left for NYC. It was beautiful in so many ways, but I never thought of it as much more than that. I remember Cooper saying he thought it would be a good thing to experience everything because that's what someone who wants to write should do. But I'm not sure that I buy it.

There are a lot of hippies in this world. Some at Earlham, and many, many in London whom I liked because they were gentle people and because I thought they understood what Love is and even what Beauty is but perhaps at the expense of work and dignity and a lot of things of value.

It's probably easier to ignore the whole thing and just live straight. That is take everything you are handed by society and confront only what doesn't make sense. Alternatively, it may be easier drift into that multi-colored void in which everything is all right and whatever you do (or fail to do) is cool. In any case, I find it hard to write a letter and not sound high-handed. Your description of the scenes back home provoked much in me. I wish I were there to sit down and talk with you and Jay and Bernie and Bob about all the stuff you can't really say in a letter—especially one that isn't likely to get there for weeks. In the meantime, I will continue to worry while hoping for the best.

I've met people from all over at the work camp here. A few of us are going on to the Pyrenees together. When I find out where I'm going, I will send you an address. Send me Bob's address. I wrote him and Jay this letter one lonely night about a week or two ago hoping I'd hear from them when I got to Paris. But I sent it to Jay's parents' address, so maybe he never got it.

Traveling in Europe is mostly a great high. There are so many fantastic sights to absorb, and I like the way people live here. But there are times when the high I feel one day leads to a precipitous drop the next. It's good to stop for a while. But weary or not, I want to touch and feel as many things as I possibly can.
Pete

While I was in Europe, Larry, Jay and Cooper were boarding a jet for San Francisco. It was the Summer of Love and the scene of drug-fueled gatherings of flower children. Ken Kesey, Neal Cassady and their entourage of dopesters, runaways, musicians and poets were rambling around with the Merry Pranksters on the Electric Kool-Aid Acid bus, brain-soaked on LSD. The best rock musicians of our generation were blasting out chords at the Fillmore West and the Avalon Ballroom, playing concerts publicized on mind-bending, crazy-colored psychedelic posters stapled to telephone poles and pasted onto walls all around the city.

After landing at SFO, they made a beeline to Golden Gate Park where they encountered George Harrison, who was trying to take an inconspicuous walk. He was immediately engulfed by an adoring mob. Somebody handed him a guitar. He played a few songs and plotted a means of escape.

The next day, they scored three kilos of grass, packed it into Jay's Army-issued duffel bag and sent it home on a Greyhound bus. Later they hitchhiked to see Jay's Uncle Morris at his ranch outside of Sacramento. Morris was taken aback by the sight of his long-haired nephew and his scruffy sidekicks. In the end, he attributed the transformation of his nephew to the car accident in which Jay's head broke the steering wheel of the Impala. "It was the hit on his head that turned him into a hippie," Morris concluded.

The next day, it took them three rides to get from the ranch to Laguna Beach where they ate baloney sandwiches on a sun-bleached hillside overlooking the freeway. "Life doesn't get any better than this," Larry declared.

The next ride took them to Ensenada, where they imbibed vast quantities of tequila. On the way back to California, they stopped in Tijuana and bought cheap Mexican ponchos and switchblade knives.

A Mexican family took them as far as San Diego in the back of a blue El Camino. Just as they hopped off, a California state patrol car roared up. Within seconds they were spread-eagled against the trunk of the patrol car. As the two cops frisked Larry and Jay, Cooper tossed his knife into a bed of cacti. He waved goodbye to his compadres as they were hauled away.

Larry and Jay spent the night in the San Diego jail. They watched the boats come into the harbor as the sun went down over Coronado Bay. They recounted the scenes they recalled from *Cool Hand Luke* and wondered if they would survive the night. While Jay slept, Larry breakfasted on the white bread, prunes and coffee that was shoved into the cell. An hour later, the guard rattled the bars, opened the door, and told them, "You guys are free. Just make sure you get the hell out of town and I mean now." They stumbled out of the jail and squinting in the California sunlight beheld Cooper who had spent the night at the bus station. "Guys," Cooper said, "The Dead are playing tonight. We have to go see them. "Not us," Jay told him. We are hightailing the hell out of here."

As my friends were making their way back from California to Maryland, I was hitchhiking through Spain, stopping along the way in San Sebastian, Madrid and Barcelona.

12 Agosto 1967 (letter from PB to LH)

Barcelona

Larry,

I'm three flights of stairs up from the Calle Condell—an alleyway crammed with bars and bodegas and wine shops. I'm sitting in a blank-walled brownish room just bigger than the bed. The room has two windows that open onto interior hallways and one small one to the outside. I'm smoking a Chesterfield, having just drunk half a bottle of Pantavin Blanco. I'm in Barcelona where it is hot and steamy, and there's no ventilation in my room. The water in the tap comes and goes. I'm a long way from home and I haven't eaten for 24 hours. But I'm crazy happy. There's this girl. She's blonde and German. Her name is Ursula.

I met Ursula in Madrid I was at the youth hostel when I was doing nothing except aimlessly blowing up a bota bag when two German girls appeared. They had hitched together from Germany, and were apparently about to part ways because one of them was into a French cat. They argued on and on while I sat there reading a story in the Saturday Evening Post titled: Why the Beatles Will Not Return. I finished the article and looked up to see a petite green-eyed blonde girl, turn to me and say:

"You hitchhike to Barcelona with me?"

"Yes!" I say (fuck yes).

I wish you could see her. I really do. I wish you could see her smile and laugh. She laughs with her eyes.

The next day, we are on the road that goes across northern Spain to Barcelona. Ursula is a master. She hitchhikes with her entire body and femininity. As a result we never waited more than 10 minutes for a ride in Spain where the hitching was said to be virtually impossible—that is worse than in the United States. We are picked up by a series of vacationers, businessmen and truck drivers. Either she speaks to them in her halting Spanish, or I do in a mixture of English and French.

The road from Madrid to Barcelona is the best one in Spain, but it's still impossible to go very fast. It winds down the sides of mountains and descends into small towns. The way is very beautiful with its kaleidoscope colors of red dirt, golden fields of wheat and hay, and dark patches of green where grapes are grown for wine. Spain is a country of open plains and cloudless skies as blue as the Mediterranean. But it is terribly poor. There were many times when we passed small villages with houses the color of the dirt. They seem frail or inconsequential as though a strong, sand-heavy wind might knock them down. Yet somehow, they endure.

We drive by farmers working in the fields or making their way down the roads with their overloaded donkeys or mules. It seems stark and lonely, but there is music in the wind that blows across the fields.

After hitching all night, we come to Barcelona. We find a tiny hotel and crash. Later, in the afternoon when Spain is asleep, she comes to my room. She is fresh from a shower and smells like the fields of lavender we passed in the night. For a few happy, funny minutes we tell each other about who we are and where we have come from, but it's mostly silly because I understand no German outside of words like knockwurst and sauerkraut, and because she really understands very little English.

We laugh, and hold each other and kiss. Slowly, at a pace that is suitable to this southern clime, we shed our clothes and explore our bodies. In minutes we are sweltering and soaking in our mutual sweat, but it is lovely and intoxicating. But suddenly, to my utter dismay, she pulls away.

"No," she says, and starts to cry on the verge of tears. Was it something I said or did? No, no, she says and then explains (as best as I could understand) that she had been pregnant once and wasn't now and how in a dream her child had asked, "Why did you dead me?" I suddenly felt really bad. But even if I spoke perfect German, I still wouldn't have known what to say or how to say it.

I dig her and we are going to travel together to Hamburg or maybe even to the town where she lives. If it works out, maybe I will stay a bit with her. If not, I will head north to see Ulf—the Swedish guy I met at the work camp in France. He lives in Goteborg, and he told me I should come to visit if I ever came his way.
Pete

I traveled with Ursula from Barcelona to Marseilles and north through Switzerland to Germany, hitchhiking all the way. It was not easy to get a ride. Sometimes there were so many travelers lined up at the on ramps to the freeways that we had to wait your turn. There were times when I resorted to standing well off the road so that it appeared to unsuspecting drivers that Ursula was travelling alone. They would roar to a stop, then I would come running up, packs in hand. It wasn't something I'm proud of.

We parted in Hamburg, after meeting her friends and spending an evening at a bar on the Reeperbahn. She was back in her element. It was time for me to go. She helped me buy a train ticket to Denmark, then said good bye.

Leaving Hamburg, I was alone for the first time since departing from London Even then, it was less than an hour before I joined up with Heinrich, a German soldier, who was also on his way to Paris. It was an unsettling feeling, less one of loneliness than of loss. I guessed I was just feeling the weight of separation from everyone I had ever known and loved, some of whom, like Ursula, I knew I would never see again.

I thought about how Ursula was feeling and how she was haunted by an image of a child she never knew and who existed only in her sadness. I had kissed her tears, and felt as close to her at that moment as I ever had to anyone. But once we got to Marseilles, our connection started to slip away, and it all but vanished by the time we reached Hamburg. I wondered if that would always be the way. Would I ever find someone to hold fast?

I spent my last two weeks in Europe exploring Copenhagen, Goteborg (where I stayed with Ulf and his family) and Amsterdam. I stayed the final night in Paris in a *pension* not wanting to go.

Mom and Dad were relieved to see me descend from the plane at National Airport. They liked knowing their children were safe and secure. Six months was a long time to go without a visit or even a phone call. But any anxiety they had expended on me paled compared to their worry over Dick. He had been in Vietnam for more than a year. Although he wrote regularly, they knew that the conditions there were changing so quickly that by the time they heard any news, everything might have changed. Dad was a constant worrier and suffered his eldest son's absence. Yet he was at peace. In a letter to Dick he wrote:

> *I was greatly moved by your letter. I must confess I had the same choking feeling I had on the day I tried to say goodbye to you almost a year ago. In a sense, I was again saying goodbye to a boy facing a great adventure, uncertainly but with quiet courage and idealism. Now I am seeing a man who*

too soon perhaps has come face to face with the human race's great dilemma—the pull toward the material that leads to self-destruction and the pull toward spiritual transformation that comes from the heritage of men like Bach, Mozart, Einstein, Shakespeare and so many, many more. In Vietnam it is not easy to keep the focus on the latter but, as you wrote, the Vietnamese have learned to endure hardship and at the same time achieve inner peace.

No matter how discouraging things are, there is one great driving force that keeps us going—the necessity of making a better world for our children. Or for making our children more capable of finding a measure of happiness even in the world as it exists today. Despite your discouragement, we know that you have too much to offer to give way, including the gift of compassion and the ability to convey it in words.

I was also happy to find Dick's response to a letter I had sent him several months before.

Dear Pete

I was not surprised about your interest in pacifism since it is something that has been on my mind for quite some time. It is impossible to follow this war and the daily fortunes of the Vietnamese people without being appalled at what the use of guns brings not only in terms of human suffering but in terms of the eroding of the mind that accompanies such use.

I have met soldiers deeply affected from having to kill even once. Their pain may continue for many years to come. But all too often I have met soldiers reduced to almost a primitive mentality—no longer capable of seeing the enemy as human beings and taking sadistic pleasure in massacre.

Life is cheap when war is used as a matter of public policy, and the effects of this war will carry on far beyond the time when the last shot is fired.

One thing is fairly evident. I could never fight in this war. But I am still not sure that this qualifies me as a pacifist. At times I find myself very un-pacifistic, with all my wrath directed toward the American side. I find myself combing through the newspapers for VC victories—based on my belief that they have a rightful claim to victory—which is usually measured by the number of American soldiers killed.

Every act of war is upsetting, but I have not really gone through the long self-analysis needed to come up with a firm conviction. It doesn't really make any difference to me whether I am legally registered as a pacifist although it would certainly be nice to know that my present activity would take the place of the draft.

I agree with you that it is probably necessary to start thinking about this now. You have a lot of thinking to do. With the war currently raging in Vietnam, and the prospect of World War III greatly increased with a possible US-Soviet confrontation near the Gulf of Aqaba, you have to decide how much your views are based on a particularly unjust war or on the traditional pacifist code.

It's possible that you not having the support of church doctrine could make it rough going since people sometimes find it hard to understand that morality can exist outside religion.

The best way to clarify your views and strengthen your defense when the time comes may be to arrange a series of interviews or discussions with professors and church officials. It could be a good way of making sure of your beliefs and discovering just how wide a commitment you are willing to make. I would like to hear more about your ideas as they become formulated.

Dick

Chapter 10

It was evident after returning to Earlham that I had missed a great deal, and most notably the invasion of the counterculture. Flowered shirts, bell-bottoms and sandals were in. Even the jocks were wearing love beads. Not all of them, but at least one or two.

September 29, 1967 (letter from PB to LH)

Dear Larry,

We were sitting around last Saturday sipping bourbon. We finished it, and Lucy asked me if I had any grass. I said I did. We all went upstairs and rolled a joint. Lucy smoked some. I smoked some. Roy, who had not previously smoked grass, smoked as well. Amy, a "straight-grub" did not. Lucy was stoned in about five minutes. Roy didn't feel anything. Amy went downstairs and read a magazine. I got pretty high. We played word games for a couple of hours and everything was very funny. Lucy fell down the stairs not once but twice but she wasn't hurt.

I came back from England excited about my new jargon—spacing out, blowing your mind, freaking out, uptight, etc. etc.—but everyone is already using it ad nausea. In the Commons one day, Bill France who now prefers to be called Sunshine asked me what I'm into. "Into?" I say, "I don't know. This shirt I guess." I know I was supposed to say Zen Buddhism or Hatha Yoga or weaving or something, but I just couldn't do it.

I talked to Jay some after you left. He told me a lot about trying not to get uptight so often. Then we went to his house and there were some strange guys in the house cooking grass in the oven, which as you might guess, made him uptight in the extreme. Then he got even more uptight with Cooper because Cooper wasn't getting uptight at all.

I just finished this novel by Heinrich Boll called The Clown. You should pick it up when you get the chance. Also I'd like you to send me Ochsman's address, if you have it or can get it. I called him a couple of times after you left only to find out that he'd left for North Carolina four days before. I'd really like to write him.

We got this house off-campus. I'm living in it with Roy and Brad. We all cook breakfasts and dinners (mostly beans and cheese) and worry about the gas bill and who is going to run downstairs to light the pilot on the water heater. It's pretty huge compared to what I expected (Roy found it while I was in Europe). We each have our own room, and there's a big kitchen, living room, bathroom and an attic. I've got everything I need. What I needed more than anything was some space, and now I've got it. Write soon.

Pete

On campuses and throughout the country, resistance to the war was building. On October 21, 100,000 people descended on Washington for a mass demonstration organized by the National Committee to End the War in Vietnam. Dr. Benjamin Spock and David Dellinger spoke, saying it was time to shift from protest to resistance. After the rally, about half the crowd marched to Foggy Bottom where Allen Ginsberg, Abbie Hoffman and the Fugs led chants aimed at levitating the Pentagon and exorcising the evil within. It was pure lunacy. But then, so too was the war.

October 21, 1967 (letter from PB to LH)

Larry

I have on my walls a long note that Nancy Slonim (the teen-visionary) gave me one day in Advanced Grammar and Composition class. Halfway down the page it commands: "Be in love with your life." I think I am at least for this moment. It's a rare strange and weird feeling given the many things to anguish over. Our house leaks heat, and there is a constant northeasterly gale coming through my closed bedroom window.

People say I laugh a lot and want to know my secret. I do and I don't know what it is. I do get terribly depressed though about wasting time and about stimulus deprivation (Intro to Psych taught me to say things like that). Perhaps when I get up the nerve, I will take a cold bath. I believe a lot of people ought to see a good Greek tragedy at least once a week. I daydream a lot about people and places in Europe.

I just received this very serious letter from you which sets me to thinking about how we really ought to put our minds together and, tedious as it may be, go through a very detailed and objective analysis of the first two decades of our existence, simply because life has been seeming so strange and inexplicable of late, and I desperately want to make sense of it all.

I decided to write to Bob a few weeks ago. I was feeling bad that I did not talk to him when he was home. It was kind of disturbing to see him as so distant from everything he has been a part of for so long. So I thought it to be proper and necessary for the sake of the eternal extenuation of our friendship to write him and explain all and make sense of everything.

However, papers bogged me down and after a while I thought that it wasn't worth it. All things have to end sometime. I've somehow reached the point where I feel we've done all we possibly could for Jay, spurring him to celebrated highlights as a studious musician, introducing him to the magic of Crime and Punishment, and rational-empiricism, inspiring greatness. It's time for each of us to step out and do Great Things. What the hell, let's not make immortal old things and cling to them in fear of new ones. There must be new ones somewhere. Something beyond sex, booze, drugs, fast cars and kidding ourselves into thinking that we will become accomplished at something without even trying which is exactly what we are doing.

Anyway you are cordially invited to a Thanksgiving feast at my ramshackle house. My parents sent $25 for food and drink, so I could even pay for most of your gasoline if you can come. Call me around midnight (collect-house to house) some time so we can figure it out.
Please send recipes.
Pete

Larry took me up on my invitation and hitchhiked to Earlham, which was a straight shot on I-70 from Towson College. Never mind that it was November and bitterly cold. Hours after leaving Towson, he was left on the shoulder of the poorly lit freeway in Wheeling, West Virginia. Snow began to accumulate. He became increasingly pitiful until some cops came by and gave him a ride to the edge of town. He made it as far as Zanesville, Ohio where he spent the night in a 24 – hour laundromat.

He arrived just as I was sitting down to a turkey dinner with Kathy, Brad, Roy, our roommate Rolf and some other friends. We were thrilled to welcome the weary traveler to our table. Over the next three days, he regaled us with the details of his journey and misadventures at home. It made our lives in Quakerville seem bland. We had long, boozy conversations about the purpose of life, and encouraged him to transfer to Earlham and move into our attic. But good sense prevailed, and he steeled himself for the return 500 mile journey home. We were going to take him to the closest on-ramp to I-70, but instead we pooled our funds and bought him a ticket on a Greyhound Bus.

By the beginning of the New Year, American and South Vietnamese forces were faltering badly. In January, the North Vietnamese Army and Viet Cong launched the Tet offensive that struck more than 100 cities and villages. The city of Hue was besieged for more than a month. Thousands of residents were executed, and the city was all but destroyed

The strength of the opposition, and the shift in attacks from the jungles to the cities came as a shock. The Viet Cong even took over the American embassy for a few hours. The next day, newspapers posted a picture of a South Vietnamese official executing a Viet Cong prisoner on the street in Saigon at point-blank range. It was a revolting image that made you question the side we were on. One more reason why supporting the war was untenable.

January 15, 1968 (letter from LH to PB)

Pete,

There have been a few setbacks of late. I got a note on official yellow paper placed in my P.O. box, (no doubt by a man in a trench coat and pearl gray sunglasses) that said I owe $100 in overdue parking tickets. If don't pay them I'll never see my grades.

Besides that is an appalling lack of love—retraction there's plenty of love—it's just emanating from the wrong direction. I love fully 73 percent of the entire female world. I love them truly and tenderly. Some I want for screwing, but some for fondling, some for kissing, some for holding tightly

in the night while I rage and weep, some for their smell, others for their eyes or legs or hair or laugh or walk or smile or breasts or calves (did you ever notice, mon frere, how huge the correlation is between the lack of love and sex and an increase in attention paid to chicks).

Did you ever notice how nice girls are in so many very and subtle ways like their stockinged or tights-covered legs, and that area right behind the knee that is always soft and clean and smooth? Or how they smile at a joke or laugh unselfconsciously. Or when you trace the length of their silky smooth warm- smelling dark hair, not very dark not blonde sort of changeling brown (as it slips against their milky cheeks or maybe as a strand of it lays on a pink, wet corner of their lip) or in the way they just unthinkingly toss their hair with their hand sort of impatiently.

Oh man. Where are the girls who will hold me, caress the back of my tired neck, giggle at my antics and tales, unhesitatingly kiss me full on the mouth in public, tenderly lean against my chest and fall asleep with her long dark hair spread on my pillow? Where, for chrissake is love?

Next term looms as a more promising adventure. Randy and I are getting an apartment (a _pad_ man). Plus I will be taking lovely and exciting courses with pounds of novels to read and dreams of papers to write. Oh joy.

Otherwise my life is interspersed with short lived moments of dissatisfaction, loneliness, wholesale alienation and angst. Please tell Roy, Rolf and Brad that I miss them and the house and Cream being played constantly and tacos and rainy afternoons. And of course convey special messages of affection to your sister and to Lucy (how that name comes up mixing memory and desire) and Amy Joy and other friends and moments that I think of often late at night when I'm alone.

Please write, I also miss you.

Larry

February 2, 1968 (letter from PB to LH)
Larry,

Sorry this letter is so long in coming. I hope you got my latest attempt at a short story. I'm still awaiting your suggestions or scathing review. I have been trying to decide on a title and have thought of several including: Perishable. Abandon If Not Delivered after Ten Days; Daddy Warbucks and the Space Age; or simply, The Recent but Unheralded Death of Modern Man. If it's the latter, I will introduce the story with an obituary describing how Modern Man slipped in the bathtub and cracked his head on the faucet. The irony was that he had just bought one of those rubber bath mats but left it in the backseat of his car.

That aside, I'm about halfway through Winter Term (Medieval Poetry, Shakespeare, and Philosophy from Hegel to Heidegger. The last one blows me away).

Also, I'm reminded how we had once talked about growing up and becoming twenty, and the necessity for reexamining our lives at that date. I think two key themes would come up. The first is that we read a lot of books. The second is that we always thought we would be Somebody by now.

I'm pretty sure that all that reading helped expand our minds and therefore our world. After all, what is more real than whatever is going on in your head? As to the second point, I always hoped to become the next Tolstoy or Scott Fitzgerald, Bosley Crowther or Jimmy Breslin. It's terrible to find out I'm not and never will be. But what the hell. We only ever become who we are. And where you end up doesn't even matter as much as the process it took to get there.

When I saw you last you told me that what you really want to do is stop worrying about the whole damn mess, have four kids, watch football with a beer in your hand and just enjoy it. But I couldn't take you seriously simply because neither of us is able to accept things as they are. Nor could we ever see financial success as actually meaning anything or wall-to-wall carpeting as a value. After all, you can't even get through college without questioning the sense of it all. Whatever we ultimately choose to be or do has to be on our own terms.

I don't know what else to say except write back immediately.

Pete

February 5, 1968 (LH to PB)

Pete

The story I like. I mean I like it and I liked (more than I can say) your sending it to me like that and I like your saying that you wanted my comments. I thought these three things: I'm always so aware of your precision and discipline and care when I read your fiction. This story (which *was good. Transition very good. Last scene o.k., conversation in the kitchen very nice) was too short. I wanted more particularly after the flashback which made me expect more. But it was good!*

A stray thought. All of the 20th century modern American writers felt that no authority (society, church, convention, morality, etc.) was any longer valid. They all looked inwardly and from this void (unlike the Romantics, they thought nature was nowhere) they created great literature, prose and poetry alike. So the message must be that when you stand in front of a mirror that reflects only your image (no bookcases or windows or walls thick with posters and backwards writing and no corners or ceilings) when all you see is yourself and you like it (after a good long probing look) then you are all the way home, free and clear, Willie, free and clear.

Films: Chappaqua, Exterminating Angel. Cheap meal: Tuna noodle casserole.

Larry

March 11th 1968 (letter from LH to PB)

Dear DC (diligent correspondent),

There seems to be a breakdown in communication in this relationship based on your exasperating inability to write a fucking letter once in a while. So not to stand on ceremony, I begin this epistle.

School is becoming a multi-level answer for a myriad of questions. I enjoy classes, books, discussions, papers, and coffee breaks with professors and all the rest that school means. But I also grow more aware that school is a microcosm of nothing that I can recognize in the real world except maybe bigger and more sophisticated schools. School is proving to be a four-year vacation condescendingly given by the Selective Service System. I had just begun to think seriously about graduate school when those plastic bastards lifted all graduate school deferments. My plans all begin after graduation (perhaps your influence) anyway I think hard about the great split after that milestone of receiving that lambskin that will bring that long-awaited tear to my mother's cheek.

Jay, amazingly, split (leaving Lorraine behind) with some insignificant little trollop in her Austin Healey. Into the night storms Our Hero in his search for sanity, peace of mind, and the great American frontier. Jay as mythic hero of the sixties. Levy as the anti-hero of a modern novel. It's sad to tell the very undramatic truth. Jay as the unhappy eternal fuck-up jumping out of the car in South Carolina one lonely night and hitchhiking back to womb-like Takoma Park. It's funny, but more than funny, it's sad, so sad.

I never talk to those cats or write them or see them anymore. But I found out Jay was in town and I was inexplicably anxious to see him. Eileen and I had gone to Dupont Circle to see some films (Black Orpheus and La Notte) and afterwards, we went to the apartment.

What ennui. What dreariness. But for my constant stream of jokes, there was no speech. Cooper gave up his classical guitar lessons and takes only nine hours for credit at school. Jay lives at home, yes home, and never, he admitted, reads or thinks or works or does anything. Tom Howell lives at the apartment and so does Snyder. They own respectively a dog and a cat. Both animals, like their owners, are mad, roughed up and ragged, homeless, scraggly and unwashed.

Naturally give my love to Lucy. Is that a love thing with her you and her? Wild rumors have reached even this far south.

I'm pissed that you haven't written so do so post-haste.

Larry Horwitz

At rallies across the country, demonstrators chanted "*Hey, Hey LBJ, how many kids did you kill today?*" It was brutal. Johnson looked old. Senator Eugene McCarthy emerged as a viable peace candidate. He was eloquent, inspiring. With the help of student volunteers who got themselves Clean for Gene, he came in a close second in the New Hampshire primary.

Lucy and I and about 25 Earlham students bussed to Wisconsin to canvass for McCarthy. We arrived late Friday night and slept on the floor of a church. The next day, we were sent to distribute fliers and urge the locals to vote for McCarthy. We were earnest and enthusiastic. But we were a motley crew, and it occurred to me that it was more likely that the local folks would shoot us than be swayed to our side.

On Sunday morning, we were visited in the campaign office by Paul Newman. Betty Comden and Adolph Green came along and sang us a song. After another day of doorbelling, we headed back to Indiana. On the way home, we heard that LBJ had announced that he wouldn't seek re-election. We cheered madly, confident that McCarthy would become the next president.

April 3, 1968 (letter from LH to PB)

Pete,

Yesterday there was an actual student demonstration centered on demands for higher salaries for Profs. Fairly cool but exactly the kind of nowhere demonstration you'd expect from Towson. Hill wants me to organize a small coterie of radicals and do something for student's rights next year. Horwitz as the latter day Mario Savio, curly black hair in the wind, jeans and boots, yellow and black striped t-shirt and leather jacket speaking to assembled crowds of following kids.

But I think and worry and cannot understand current domestic politics at all. Is it possible that everything we saw as an ill, will soon be gone, and that all that we desperately hoped for will come true? Can I trust Lyndon Johnson after all he's done? Can peace come? The Korean peace took 18 months to settle, and in the meantime twelve thousand soldiers died in the fucking mud.

My god how I don't want to die in the mud. No, I want to die in the mud sometimes but it's always as a fantastically brave underground cat on foreign soil. I wear an incredible cowboy hat, and I'm referred to as loco Americano or formidable keed and who looks amazingly like Steve McQueen, has secret lovers in the Alps waiting for my triumphant return and who says tough shit when she learns of my horribly gory brave death. And, putting on my battered hat, brought from the jungles by my Gunga Din-like sidekick, herself hoists a rifle and continues my good work, and, for full literary effect, is pregnant with my son.

Enclosed, some Towson newspaper clips, regards to Kathy and Lucky Lucy.

Larry

On April 4, Dr. Martin Luther King, Jr was assassinated at 6 p.m. as he stood on the balcony of the Lorraine Motel in Memphis. It was more devastating even than the death of JFK. King embodied the idealism and hope that drove us forward. We were inexpressibly saddened and jarred by how easily a bullet could alter history's course. I worried that without King to lead it, the civil rights movement would be taken over by leaders who were angry, radical, and violent.

Dr. King's death provoked an outpouring of rage that spilled onto the streets in Baltimore, Boston, Chicago, Detroit, Kansas City, Newark and Washington D.C. Jay was living in Takoma Park at the time and working for his father at Sam's Pawn Shop. Later that day, Jay's dad called to tell him that that the alarm had been set off. As Jay recounted:

> He asked me to go to the shop to see why it went off. By the time I got to the store, it had stopped. Everything was locked up tight. I got back on the bike and made a U-turn. Then I drove by the corner of 14th and U. There were people everywhere. Just as I got to the intersection, somebody shouted—get that white motherfucker. I turned to see who they were yelling about and realized it was me.
>
> Everything went into slow motion the way it does when you think you're about to die. I saw lots of heavy-duty brothers start to rush me. I was right across from the Tivoli Theater. The street is very wide there so there was space between us, but they were coming at me fast. I hit the throttle. The front wheel popped straight up into the air. A brother missed me by about three inches. What the fuck is going on? I really didn't know. I just blasted out of there. I didn't stop at one light all the way down Georgia Avenue. I ripped right through everything. It looked like the sky was on fire.
>
> I had no idea how widespread the rioting was. I found out that the first place hit was People's Drug Store. The door was bashed in. Everything was taken. Drugs, medical supplies and everything else was taken right off the shelves. People were walking away with all kinds of stuff.
>
> I got home safe, but when I walked into the house, Dad called and said he was coming to pick me up so we could go protect the shop. I told him that wasn't a good idea, but I couldn't talk him out of it. We drove down 15th street. By

then there were hundreds of people in the street, carrying off booze, clothes, stereos, furniture and even washing machines. I even saw one guy carry out a whole rack of sun glasses.

When we got to the shop, the place was licked clean. There was nothing left. I thought Dad was going to have a stroke.

What was really heartbreaking is that it felt like such an attack. This was before black power and all that shit. We had always gotten along with the people who live there. I loved working there. You know even before we were old enough, we used to go down to the clubs and listen to these incredible musicians hammering out these intricate riffs on Hammond B-3 organs. They always let us in. I'm an idiot. But like a million other Jews, I felt we were in it together. There were a lot of Jews who were active in the civil rights movement. And why not? Jews have been kicked around for a thousand years. They know about that shit. I have to say, all that anger took me by surprise.

Stokely Carmichael tried without success to calm the crowd and channel its anger into protest. The destruction went on into the night. Windows were smashed. Stores were vandalized. There were fires everywhere. Many of the firemen and police who rushed to the scene were pelted with rocks and bricks.

The city smoldered for days. All told, 150 fires had been set, 1,000 buildings were destroyed or damaged, and twelve people were killed. A lot more might have been if were up to J. Edgar Hoover. He was pressing Mayor Washington to order the police to shoot the rioters. But Washington refused.

The community was devastated. Those who could, moved away. Nobody, not the city, the federal government or the banks, was willing to invest in rebuilding. It made bad conditions even worse, and the detritus from the riot was left there long after the rioting was over.

April 15, 1968 (letter from PB to LH)

Larry,

I just got back from a whirlwind tour of Wisconsin. Seeing and hearing McCarthy, listening to the people voice their garbled opinions about choices that will affect generations to come. It was good for the soul, which has taken some terrible beatings lately—King getting shot, listening to black folks talk about hatred, watching white folks glut themselves with guilt, talking to Upward Bound students in Dayton put down other Negroes for rioting and looting.

Given all the potential for disaster that awakes and brushes its teeth with us and accompanies us throughout the day, I generally retreat (absurdly) into studying which mostly consists of reading comic novels (for my senior project): Gargantua and Pantagruel by Rabelais, Tristram Shandy by Laurence Sterne Roderick Random by Smollett; Miss Lonelyhearts by Nathaniel West; The Horse's Mouth by Joyce Cary, and V by Thomas Pynchon). Which is nice, great, and fantastic. Rabelais is my fave. Especially in describing Gargantua, a colossus of a man who issued from his mother's left ear in the 11th month of her labors, and bounded out crying "Drink. Drink. Drink." Gargantua subsequently fathered Pantagruel whose birth Rabelais describes in dramatic fashion:

> *For a while his mother was bringing him forth and the midwives stood by ready to receive them, there first issued from her belly 78 salt vendors; nine dromedaries bearing ham and smoked ox tongues; seven camels bearing chitterlings; 25 cart loads of the leeks, garlic, onions and chives. This terrified some midwives, but others said: "Here is good provision!"*

Needless to say his fair mother died immediately, but Gargantua consoled himself looking on his offspring. "Ha, my little son! My bollocky darling, my adorable fartlet, how lusty you are."

Rabelais goes on through five volumes offering the deluge of epithets ("By the Pope's holy scrotum stones"), odes and poetic veneration of the joyously obscene. It keeps me on an even keel.

Perhaps things are looking up. Maybe we won't have to go to Canada after all. But peace talks aren't going anywhere. I'm convinced we must work as hard as possible for McCarthy. After hearing Johnson drop out I thought about jumping on Kennedy's side, but feel an aversion to him every time I hear him talk. My respect for McCarthy is growing.

I see no reason that I cannot go see America (or Canada) this summer. I think the route farthest north, perhaps the Yukon trail, would be advised. Also curious as to Levy's physical and military status.

In vino veritas

Pete.

April 22, 1968 (letter from LH to PB)

Pete,

I saw a lot of Levy during Easter vacation and he is a difficult person these days to see a lot of. He is tall as always, extremely thin, his head full of long fly-away blonde hair that explodes out of the sides of his head. His expression is vacant and he hangs his head a lot and doesn't look at people in the eye when he talks to them. My mother almost wept when he walked in for the first time.

<u>Jay Levy</u>: Levy and I talk a lot, and I found him aware painfully aware of how incredibly fucked-up he is. I found myself unable to say much except, "Levy, you can do it, but I can't do it for you." He shrugs with resignation, looks in the sky, tries to figure it out and never does. He says he can't play good piano anymore. He lives with his parents. He has no job or anything. He was recently caught by his parents cleaning a kilo of grass in the kitchen. Quick-witted that he is, he told his mom that it was modeling clay.

<u>Bob Ochsman</u>: Levy went to see Ox but he told me later that they have a little or nothing to say to each other. Ox could never quite dig Jay's problems, hang ups or confusion. Plus Levy resents Ox for his smooth passage through life despite the fact that Levy at his best would never live his life that way. He just sees the staggering polarity between them as too much to overcome.

<u>Bernard Cooper</u>: When Cooper turned 21, he became the heir of a trust fund of $2,000 left to him by his mother. He took $1,200 out of that and immediately purchased a Norton 750cc Death Cycle that is so fast and loud and terrifying that people shut their doors in fear when Cooper rides up residential avenues. His driving permit in Maryland is totally void so he cleverly falsified his way into the possession of a D.C. permit. Cooper is

amazing and perhaps the most insane of all. His plans include an ultimate split on the cycle to the jungles of South America via the Pan-American Highway. God be with him.

As for the summer, any fucking route is cool with me. I think about Kathy a lot. Would you tell her for me? I think about your political al dente and wish you and McCarthy success. It's just that I'm afraid national politics are too big and bust for me.

Larry

Just as I thought it couldn't get worse, Robert Kennedy was murdered moments after he won the California Democratic primary. Just two months after the death of Dr. King, we were devastated again. It seemed like all efforts toward creating a better world were being thwarted by gun-wielding madmen. Instead of becoming more idealistic, democratic and just, the nation was falling into a very dark hole.

June 20th 1968 (letter from LH to PB)
Dear Pete,

First of all let me extend my apologies for being such a tardy and thoughtless letter writer. It has been a strange year all around. I finished up exams and drove home to suburban luxury where I very honestly did nothing but sleep late, take a lot of showers, read magazines, watch television and see our friends in Takoma Park.

In Cooper's apartment we have the following: Bob Barrett lives in what was once the head room and who is barely seen or heard. He prefers to play his guitar and make it with his chick, and not involve himself in any extracurricular social shit. Tommy now lives in Levy's old room, although he did leave for the west coast just a few days ago. He was recently gifted a $1,600 16-millimeter Bolex camera by a Toad Hall resident (to be discussed later). Typically, Howell is rather befuddled by the machinery and has produced nothing that we might call art but we all live in hope. Howell has no job and no visible means of staying upright and alive. His artistic caprices and good natured foolishness has turned annoying parasitism and open begging with no remnants of humility. His position has moved even the more kindly and patient members of the household to rage and disgust.

Cooper is seemingly sad. The loss of his $1,200 dollar cycle left irreparable damage to his psyche. People think he is angry or worried about things, but I think he has just had it with the scene in general. He and I have had a lot of good long honest and worthwhile talks about it. I still love him. He recently got his hair cut to a respectable business-like length, and has taken to wearing regular slacks and sports shirts and shoes <u>and</u> socks. He is studying jazz guitar with Roger and will probably get a job soon. He is still up to drugs but his disgust with the old hippie ethic is obvious. He asks for you.

On the hippie end of the street, we have Toad Hall and its newest resident, Jay Levy. Toad Hall is a huge house with about a dozen residents. The bills are all paid by this one guy who has an inheritance of about 30 million bucks. He is the same guy who gave Howell the camera and stuff. Nobody at Toad Hall works. They are all up to rock and roll music. Some of them are ex-Hangmen including Nils Lofgren, and Hangmen hangers-on. They are mostly into drugs (and I mean LSD) and promiscuous fucking. I find them a colorful and uninspiring bunch. They are all pretty concerned with being cool and uninvolved so it is hard to have anything but meaningless conversations there. They have a lot of cats (feline) and they feed them acid. The entire group travels around in a niftily decorated VW bus. They are the rage of Georgetown.

Levy seems happy, and he told me in fact that he has never been as happy as he is now. He has no job or prospects that I can discern. However, there are pianos and musicians at Toad Hall so he has that for whatever it is worth.

I hitched-hiked to Philadelphia in the broiling sun to see your lady and her friend, your sister. Both of them are on my list of top 10 human beings. Of course we had lots of a long laughing and serious discussions together. Is it love or something equally serious with you and lucky Lucy? It might as well be. She certainly is one of the finest people I know, for a million hard to describe reasons. We read books and swam in the Atlantic and went sailing on the bay and Lucy's kid brother tried to teach me how to surf. Kathy and I wandered around a bit gawking at all these giant

beachside estates that were probably worth a million dollars each. Yeah.
The rich are not like you and me.

My mother was in the hospital for a kidney stone. She's okay now. I
just thought you might want to know. Also my old nemesis, Susie, is home
and looking after me, but I've yet to see her.
I told you I thought it had been a strange year.
Larry

I stayed at Earlham during the summer to work for Upward Bound, a federal program that brought high school students from low-income families to college campuses for eight weeks. About half the students were white and came mostly from rural communities. The others were inner-city kids from Cincinnati or Dayton. Some of the Earlham professors directed the program and students like me taught, led activities and lived with the students. I had tutored some of the students during the school year but this would be a more intensive experience. It felt good to be doing something about social justice instead of just complaining.

It was a confusing time. There had been so much change. Segregation had been struck down. The courts were on the right side of history. LBJ had pushed through civil rights legislation, and he was backing it up with the War on Poverty. On the other hand, Dr. King had been shot, and George Wallace was running for president. Out in Oakland, the Black Panthers had rejected the involvement of mainstream civil rights advocates—including all whites—and were gathering arms.

In contrast, Upward Bound seemed a happy blend of school and summer camp. It was thrilling to be in a multi-racial environment, where everyone knew each other and played, laughed, argued, and shared friendships and summer crushes. Of course, after the summer, the students, except for those who were coming to Earlham, would go back to their separate places. It was exciting to get a glimpse of what the world would be like—black and white together—a few years down the road. I loved planning for classes and leading discussions, and I imagined becoming a teacher. Upward Bound gave me a new perspective. I may have wanted to be a novelist or a professor but let's face it, my talent was much too meager. Just because I admired writers, didn't mean I could be one. But that still left of lot of purposeful and gratifying things that I could pursue.

I would always write, even it wasn't anything worth preserving. I couldn't help it. My idle thoughts and daydreams were always punctuated. I imagined how they would look on paper. I'd edited in my head. I knew that Jay constantly thought about music. I could tell by looking at him. I imagined that Bob mostly meditated on matters of torque and gear ratios. I couldn't begin to guess what Cooper was thinking about. It was no mystery with Larry though. He always let you know.

July 3, 1968 (letter from PB to LH)

Dear Larry,

It is summer in Richmond, Indiana, but not too hot. I've gotten used to getting up at 7 a.m. Working at Upward Bound is hectic. Most of the students are cool. The high school chicks drive me out of my head, and I keep bumping into things when I walk. A good number of the students are high school dropouts who are on leave from a nearby Job Corps. They are some of the most interesting people—especially the ones from Chicago who love jiving us about all the streets on which you will get killed if you are white or have long hair or wear sunglasses. They also like to talk about shooting people (because there's nothing else to do) and breaking into houses and smoking "reefer."

One guy in my house has a huge scar from where he got shot in the leg. He allows how occasionally he used to shoot at people himself because they jump funny when you shoot at them. There's this white kid who calls himself Tennessee. He's from the hills, and he dropped out of school after the eighth grade. He's in my creative writing class in which I happened to read "my country tis of thee" and compared it to a representative fuckthyselfAmerica poem by Ginsberg. After which Tennessee decides to

become the next Ginsberg only with a southern drawl. Today he turned in
this poem:

> America
> Why do your sons have to fight in foreign wars?
> When will they come home?
> When will all the burning stop?
> America you are death hole
> You only know how to kill.

  I feel a bit guilty about that one but it's good to see people turned on
to poetry. Another student--a black kid from the ghetto——wrote:

> Briefly she touched the sidewalk
> As she flittered hither and yon
> Over the crusted rusted walks
> Through the pale mood pools that
> Mellowed the murky morning
> With the ripest cantaloupe covering

  I'm alternately frustrated and excited. It is definitely a job that grabs
you by the ankles every morning and shakes everything out of you by the
end of the day. Sometimes I feel I'm far more capable than I give myself
credit for. More often, I feel inadequate. I forge ahead because there is no
other choice. I have one night off a week but I'm careful not to drink or take
anything that will make me seem out of my role as a teacher/counselor/
parent to all these bloody students.

  I miss Lucy a lot and often. I've heard from her a couple of times. She's
recovered from the near pneumonia she contracted at the shore.
Pete

  After Upward Bound, Larry and I decided to hitchhike to
San Francisco to find Jay. We figured that by now he was
either living on a commune led by a psychedelic love-guru or
performing at the Fillmore West.

  We started out from Baltimore. It had rained the night
before. A steamy mist rose from the surface of the road. I was
excited and nervous. A continent stretched out before us. The
distance seemed impossibly vast. Once underway, there would
be no turning back.

We got a ride right away to New Stanton (southeast of Pittsburg) with a guy who was fresh out of college. He told us that he had put rebellion behind him and moved to the suburbs.

By noon, we were in Claysville, Pa. (pop. 702). We bought sardines, Wonder Bread and grape soda, and lunched on the bank of the Monongahela River. We got a ride with a football coach who told us that all the great NFL linemen come from there because they were sons of coal miners desperate to leave home. He took us ten miles.

We walked across a bridge and watched twenty '56 Fords fly by before a soldier driving a Pontiac Tempest with red vinyl seats and a Hurst shifter swerved to pick us up. He was making a mad dash from his wife and kids in Connecticut to his girlfriend in Colorado Springs. He was also technically AWOL from the Air Force and in a hurry to get back. *Hot damn*, we thought, *hitchhiker's gold*. Powered by amphetamines, he drove wordlessly for the next 30 hours. He stopped only when the gas tank was on empty. Each time, he told us to wake him in an hour. We reached St. Louis as the sun came up. He powered on across Missouri and Kansas through endless stretches of farmland and under a vast sky. We zipped by wheat fields and oil wells. We could have driven through six countries in Europe in the time it took us to cross the two states. When we got to Colorado Springs, the soldier had me stuff his family photos in back of the seat cushion. Then he showed us some pictures of his first true love—a Pontiac GTO.

We pulled into Colorado Springs as the light was fading. It is a fine little city, nestled in the foothills of the Rockies. Toting our knapsacks, we walked to Acacia Square where we encountered a throng of youth hanging out, doing drugs and talking about scraping up money to go to California. Most of the conversation was about speed and acid, good dope and bad trips. One of them appeared to be playing volleyball by himself without a net and without a ball. A tall, skinny, fingernail-biting, sad, lonely, going-nowhere kid showed us the way to the city park. He asked us if we thought that the hippies in Golden Gate ever littered. Some other kids came by and told how much the town sucked.

We slept under the stars, halfway to the sky. It was cold as hell. The next morning, we drank hot coffee and stood in the sunshine watching oilmen in white Stetsons drive by. We pitched stones and wondered if people ever died crossing the desert. Two Mexicans in a pickup stopped to ask us where our choppers were. They told us to climb into the back of the truck and took us to the outskirts of town. A college student named Randy pulled over. He was driving a VW bug that sounded like it was running on two cylinders. He was headed for San Francisco. Into the Rockies we climbed. The sun was bright, the air was clean. The aspens rippled, brilliant yellow against the dark green pines. We crossed the desert at night. It was cold, and it rained. We got to Reno at eight in the morning as buses and cars and RVs streamed into town. The sidewalks were crowded with tourists and panhandlers, hustlers, hookers and drunks. Inside old people played slot machines two at a time, hoping to fill up their buckets with quarters. I had never seen anything like it.

We arrived in San Francisco bleary-eyed and stiff from the long ride. We had crossed the country in seventy-two hours. We were groggy and discombobulated. Running on fumes, we walked to the corner of Haight and Asbury and then to City Lights book store hoping to bump into Lawrence Ferlinghetti. We walked through North Beach and passed the *Condor Club* where the bountiful and acrobatic Carol Doda was reputed to dance the *Twist*, the *Frog* and the *Watusi* atop a grand piano as it was lowered onto the stage. She had enormous, surgically enhanced breasts, and was the nation's most heralded topless dancer. We stopped in front of the club to admire the huge painting of her with flashing red lights where her nipples should have been.

"We really ought to check this out," Larry said.

Indeed, I thought. But they were charging ten bucks to get in (*five bucks a teat!*). Enough to live on for the next three days.

"Next time," I said. "Next time."

At last! I was in San Francisco. The Summer of Love had come and gone, but its trappings were still there—young men dressed in flowery blouses and clown-striped pants with crazy long hair, unkempt beards, bead necklaces, and hats with plumes. There were spacy but fetching girls in gauzy skirts. Singers, guitarists and pipers busked the corners, and mangy young men whispered *Grass? Acid? Speed?* as they passed by. There were bikers, junkies, runaways and prostitutes who looked like they were, as the song says, *livin' on reds, vitamin C, and cocaine*. I was a year late. As Larry put it, "By now, everyone in the Haight has pimples."

As we made our way through the city, we kept stopping to call a number we had for Jay. But it was like shouting into the void. We'd get no answer or someone would say, "Jay's not here." Once somebody said, "I'll go get him," then hung up the phone. We were starting to wonder where we would stay that night. Larry suggested we find Lorraine. Her friend Cynthia had told us she had come out here and was working at an Italian bistro in North Beach. It didn't take us long to find it. She was standing right at the hostess desk wearing a revealing silk blouse that made her look more womanly than ever, although for that matter, I had thought she was pretty womanly back when we were in junior high.

She was surprised but happy to see us. We asked about Jay.

"I'm not even talking to that bastard," she confided.

"What? You guys on the outs?"

"This time for good. I'm done."

"So no way to reach him, huh."

"I wouldn't know."

"That puts us in a bit of a bind."

"Why? You need a place to stay?"

"Well…actually."

"I'm here late tonight, but you can stay with me, if you don't mind the floor."

"Sounds perfect," Larry assured her.

She gave us her address and told us to meet her there.

"Lorraine, you're a sweetheart." I said.

It would be hours before she was home, so we made our way to the Avalon Ballroom where the *Grateful Dead* were going to play. A band named It's A Beautiful Day was singing *White bird must fly or she will die.* Then the Dead came on and started off with *Good Morning Little School Girl* and other songs from *Anthem of the Sun.* The Electric Light Company projected a shimmering backdrop of molecular shapes oozing from one to another in a way that made you think you were on acid. Jerry Garcia, all beard and granny glasses, blasted out a river of multi-colored guitar riffs. A skinny girl whirled around on stage and made me wonder which member of the band she would fuck after the concert. Jerry? Pigpen? Bob Weir? Of course, it was always Bob Weir.

After the show, we wandered the dark streets until we found Lorraine's walk-up in the Mission District, and let ourselves in. It was a one-bedroom affair, barely furnished. It was funny. I was always so sure that Jay and Lorraine would get married right after high school. He would have a steady job and she would pop out a couple of kids. They'd have a nice house in the suburbs, and everyone would be happy. I had no idea then how quickly things can change.

We were at the apartment when Lorraine got home. She took off her work clothes and put on a kimono that made us shiver with lust. She got out a bottle of Johnny Walker and poured us drinks. Pretty soon, my head was floating in the space between drunk and tired.

Loraine told us in seamy detail about how Jay left her in the lurch and was not to be trusted. Larry and I were too tired or wise to try to defend him.

"But if that's all true," Larry said, "why are you even here?"

"It's *San Francisco*, dah-ling," she said, as though that were explanation enough.

There was more to the story. A tearful rapprochement. Promises renewed. Tears shed. Coitus achieved. But there were choices to be made, neither was willing to make the right one—at least not one that the other could live with. That was it. It ended more in sadness than in rage.

By now my eyelids were drooping like a failed soufflé. We unrolled our sleeping bags. Lorraine went to bed. I woke up the next day not knowing where I was. The apartment was empty. Then Larry and Lorraine came in with coffee and bagels. On their way to get breakfast, Larry had managed to coax from her the address of Jay's last known whereabouts.

We hugged goodbye, and she told us again how much she had missed us both.

"We kind of grew up together, you know," she said.

It was true. We had been a part of the same pack of kids stumbling our way toward adulthood. She had always seemed older—preternaturally mature compared to other girls. She was lovely, charming, and unattainable. She was, and would always be, *Levy's girl*.

Thus renewed, we hiked through the city until we found ourselves standing, dumbfounded, in front of a huge, magisterial mansion in Pacific Heights. Finding Jay here seemed improbable at best. But there he was. Decked out in hippie regalia, his blond locks, long and tangled, and smiling like a madman. He told us a story about how he got there that involved an encounter with a girl named Patty while waiting in line at the Fillmore West. An all-night party. A minor break-in. It all made sense when he explained it. I mean you could see how it might have happened to Jay, if to no one else.

"Now that you're here, what do you feel like doing?" Jay asked.

"I don't know Marty, what do you feel like doing?" Larry answered. It was his stock response.

"Show us your city," I suggested.

"You got it. I'll be back in a second," he said and disappeared back into the house. We sat on the front porch, taking in the view of Fisherman's Wharf and San Francisco Bay. In a couple of minutes, he pulled up in the front of the house driving a Citroen. We had no idea where it came from, but it didn't surprise us. Somehow or other, Jay always had the coolest wheels.

The first thing he did was drive by 2400 Fulton St. where Dry Creek Road, the band Jay was in, liked to rehearse. It was an enormous white Georgian style mansion with pillars, porticos and elevated porches. It was across the street from Golden Gate Park. It had been bought by Jefferson Airplane and turned into a combination crash pad, music studio and pharmaceutical emporium that featured voluminous tanks of nitrous oxide. A contemporary version of Bosch's *Garden of Earthly Delights*.

After that, we crossed the Golden Gate Bridge into Marin County. We stopped in Sausalito, then ventured up a winding road bordered by eucalyptus trees to Mt. Tamalpais in the Marin Hills. We could see San Francisco to the south and the Pacific Ocean to the west. It was my first glimpse of it since I was ten years old. I surveyed the vast blue sky, breathed in the salty air, and soaked up the sun. *Oh California!*

Jay filled us in on his recent adventures. Landing in the city. Falling into the music scene. An unexpected reunion with Eric Baarslag at the San Francisco Art Institute. Reconnecting with Lorraine. The final break-up. A new start.

After hearing the whole story, Larry felt compelled to ask: "But Jay, when it comes down to it, you are more or less jobless, homeless and alone. Is this how you really want to live?"

"Well now that you put it that way. I guess I could go back to community college and become an accountant or a neurosurgeon."

"Seriously Jay. I'm worried about you," Larry persisted. "Tell me how are you are really feeling?"

"Horwitz, you're asking me how I do I feel?"

"Yeah. How *do* you feel?"

"Well sir," he said with a straight face. "All I can say is if I were a bell I'd be ringing."

Then he jumped up and sang a couple of choruses from *Guys and Dolls*. It was just like Jay. He would never give you a straight answer.

The trip home wasn't nearly as quick as our journey west. We got a ride out of San Francisco in a crowded Volkswagen bus. We stopped in Reno and drank free gin and tonics. But we were summarily dropped off in Salt Lake City because the driver didn't think the van could carry us all over the Rockies. After that it was a ride here and there with long periods in between. In Davenport Iowa, we met a runaway kid who spent the nights in a sewer pipe. "It's not bad," he told us. "You have to get out pretty fast when somebody flushes. But you can hear it coming in plenty of time."

The day grew long, and traffic scarce. Any hope of getting out of Iowa that night was dissipating. There we were, stranded in the middle of the country, sitting on the shoulder of the highway beside a dusty cornfield. A couple of cars barreled past but none stopped. It was getting dark, and we were down to our last cigarette.

"Fuck," I said, "What's today?"

"I don't know. Monday?

"No, I mean the date. I think it's my birthday."

"Fuck'n A. You're 21! You're legal now."

"Yeah. Big night, right?"

To celebrate, we scraped the bottom of our back packs and fished out the last Hershey Bar.

"It's all yours, Happy Birthday."

I broke it two and gave him half. It was stale and grainy, but still sweet. "It's too weird," I said. "I'm 21. We should be ordering cocktails at the Shoreham Hotel. Instead, we're stranded in the middle of Iowa."

Larry agreed. "It's anti-climactic. We oughta be doing something amazing by now, not just waiting for school to start. I mean, take Benjamin Franklin. He probably invented electricity by the time he was 21."

"I don't think anyone actually invented electricity. I'm pretty sure it's always been around."

"I'm just saying. This is not what I imagined. We're in the middle of nowhere. Levy is on a strange trip to god-knows-where. All Cooper talks about is getting lost in North Africa or moving to some desert island."

"Is it a desert island or a deserted Island? Or maybe a dessert island? I never know which."

"And Bob? Who the hell knows? We've completely lost touch. But whatever he's doing, you can it expect it will be safe and respectable and highly remunerated."

"So life is good?"

"No. Everything sucks."

"You are right about that. You saw it in Haight-Asbury, all the love is gone."

"And look at the war. We are still in that fucking thing."

"And politics? No Kennedy. No McCarthy. It's going to be Humphrey or Nixon."

"And the Panthers are taking up arms. No more Mr. Nice Guy."

"And the Yippies and the anarchists are hijacking the peace movement."

"You're right. Everything does suck."

"You sure there aren't any more cigarettes?"

"I told you we already smoked the last one."

"That's what really sucks. "

We spent the night next to a drainage ditch on the side of the road. It was just us and the crickets and snakes that were hiding in the grass. In the morning we were rescued by a travelling salesman. "The main thing you need to know is that everything that's first class in Davenport, is third-rate," he said.

We thought about extending our trip to go to the Democratic Convention, but we were done with being on the road. A slew of groups were planning to create as much havoc as possible. Mayor Daley was gearing up for a confrontation that would turn the planned coronation of Hubert Humphrey, into a sideshow. Kennedy was dead. McCarthy was losing ground. The prospects for the election were depressing. The Republicans had already nominated Nixon. I was finding it hard to imagine voting at all—even though it was the first time I could even vote.

Our next ride took us past Chicago, all the way to Cleveland. We had $30 between us. Enough for two student stand-by tickets to Baltimore. So we ended up flying the last leg and watching the convention from home.

The Yippies, as promised, were provocative, and the police reacted in full fury. The protestors were camping in Grant Park. Mayor Daley sent out 20,000 police officers (two for every one protestor) to guard them. For the next several days, the TV screens jumped from the chaos inside the convention to demonstrators being beaten by Chicago's finest. I was stunned by the level of police violence unleashed on the young white protestors. Of course, we wouldn't have been so shocked had they been black.

Chapter 11

One more year to wrap up college and determine my destiny. It was only a matter of months before I would be drafted. I was still deciding which path to follow. Graduate school? The Peace Corps? Enlist or resist? I looked everywhere for answers. We were all in the same boat, and intense quarrels about the right thing to do went late on into the night. Everyone had their own perspective. Several spelled theirs out in a campus magazine called The Prism.

Roger Ide decided to enlist in the Air Force. He wasn't trying to be a hero. He just figured that volunteering would actually reduce the likelihood of getting sent to Viet Nam. He didn't want to participate in the war but neither did he want to go to jail or Canada, "thereby cutting the umbilical cord to who I am and what I know," he wrote. "I favor a non-revolutionary path to change by working within the existing system, fault-ridden though it may be."

James Auler dropped out of Earlham during his freshman year and was reclassified 1-A. He applied for C.O. status but his application was rejected, and he was drafted. He wrote:

> I must admit, I enjoyed basic training—crawling through the mud, scrambling over rocks and shooting a rifle. There was the instructor's constant reminder that we were all going to be fighting hand to hand with Victor Charlie (the V.C.). It was not until the end of basic training, when I learned that I was assigned to become a medical corpsman instead of infantryman, that the magnitude of my indoctrination hit me. I had been preparing myself to kill. The discovery that I would not be sent to fight gave me the time and perspective from which to begin to observe the enormity of the dehumanization I had undergone. I started learning to have a

*conscience again. I suddenly realized how much a game basic
training had been for me and what dire actions this training
had led me to be blindly willing to perform.*

Pete Johnson wrote:

*I can't see what we are fighting for in Viet Nam. It seems like
it is another example of the white man's attempt to control
and manipulate non-whites. The way I see it, there are two
wars that are raging that are a thousand miles apart but are
closely related. If I must choose, I will choose to fight in the
ghettos against white imperialists. I am not afraid to take up
arms, but if do it will be for the cause of freedom, not
suppression.*

Timothy Zimmer rejected his student deferment and was
classified 1-A. After refusing induction, he was sentenced to
three years in prison.

*What I believe and propose in a way transcends reform and
revolution in seeking to establish a new and encompassing
principle, namely non-violence, which repudiates all previous
standards by which social and political change has been
judged. "Keep thyself first in peace and then thou wilt be able
to bring others to peace."*

September 25, 1968 (letter from LH to PB)

My friend,

*It seems that at the beginning of each term I write a letter describing
my courses and professors and my mental condition. So rather than go
through any strange unsettling changes in modus operandi, I will tell you
that I am taking the following:*

*<u>Race and Cultural Relations</u> taught by this tiny Jewish chick from
Berkeley campus who knows her stuff pretty well, but is real young and new
to teaching.*

*<u>Major American Poetry</u> taught by a drill sergeant who is dry and
poetry-destroying. When he speaks, I think of skeletons clattering in a cold
wind. I'm also taking <u>Literary Criticism</u> taught by the pride and joy of
Towson—the famous and revered J. Frank Guess who undoubtedly has the
tightest ass in the whole university system.*

<u>Imaginative Writing</u> taught by this effete young midget who impresses me as a guy with a lot on the ball. He read my journal replete with soul searching conversations, records of acid trips, the story of my first trip to San Francisco and tons of other madness, poetry, short stories, real life adventures, transcripts of sessions with my mother and you and the local truck driver, and every other fucking thing. Anyway, he wrote all these comments which said in kind that I was an unbelievably adroit young wordsmith, obviously serious about my writing and a shoo-in for the fame and honor that my talent so richly deserves. I swear to you he compared me to Christopher Isherwood, Jack Kerouac and Thomas Wolfe (or maybe it was Virginia Woolf. Needless to say that thrills the shit out of me.

Cooper (madman and poet). I'll never cease being delighted and amazed by him. He is fantastic for a myriad of reasons you already know. He got a job in Towson as the foreman of the 8 a.m. to 4 p.m. shift at the Glass Soda Straw Factory. He owns a 1966 triumph 500 with metallic blue paint job and ape-hangers. He is the coolest of the cool. I adore him. He purchases delicacies for our larder and wreaks havoc on my attempts at budget and meal planning. He says that he has a lot of money and we might as well live well as long as he can afford it. He is right of course. He's always right if you listen carefully.

I got a letter from Jay Levy. The letter was postmarked Sausalito and when I opened it, it said stuff like this: "Things are fine here in Des Moines Iowa landed my first big job at the Sears Roebuck. I got a nice little efficiency in a place called Punch Card Manor, and I bought a Mustang." It never broke into another style so I was duly amused but got no real information. His address is 410 Johnson Street, Sausalito California. Give it a try, why don't you?

I'm very tired of typing right now but I have much news and many tales to tell you. Please give my regards to various friends your roommates and of course love to Kathleen. Have you heard from lady love Lucy? I need her mailing address.

Larry

October 9, 1968 (letter from PB to LH)

Larry,

Now that we are seniors, we should consider the grave implications of our getting on in years. Keats at our age had but seven to go. He used most of them unwisely writing outdated poetry. There is so much to be done.

We've yet to fertilize a single egg or make anyone's belly swell. Fish and small insects do it at a ridiculously young age—having the foresight to strive for immortality while the getting is good. Our lives to date are but a series of small battles. We have yet to win a single war (not even a paltry one). Nor engineered a single successful siege. Napoleon would surely be dismayed, and as for a Rear Admiral Hornblower, we should not expect even a cheerful tut-tut.

In days of yore when old Anaximander was tripping barefoot over the Spartan plains, he came upon an old man (Heraclitus) laying in a fetal position in the midst of nowhere with his thumb up his rectum. He was grinning but shivering slightly as there was a chill in the air. Now Anaximander, being well versed in the prophets of antiquity and acquainted with Heraclitus' thesis that everything flows, did not ask why his thumb was up his ass, but rather merely inquired as to the next outpost ahead where he may, perchance, acquire a spot of tonic. He was however incredulous at the old man's somewhat garbled reply: "Wait here and it will come to you."

So it all adds up in the end. You have your choice and all, and you take the inner road out. Sisyphus rolls his rock up the hill. Demosthenes shoves a tub around because he feels like he ought to be doing something.

The only thing I've done is to take the GRE's and sent my scores to NYU at Stony Brook. I don't know much about it except that it's somewhere close to New York City.

Things don't change much here. But there is a fresh crop of freshmen girls. Somehow they don't seem quite as virginal as when I first arrived. I think it's likely that they are part of a new wave of hip high school chicks who've been turning on for years. It makes me feel old.

The whole rhetoric of politics (and the constant talk about what if Wallace runs, what we all should do and how fucked up this country is, etc. etc.) is starting to sound tiresome and meaningless. Sometimes I think that no matter what we do in life, everything will go on the same. The Draft is still the only thing that actually brings the real world creeping in to our collective consciousness.

Enjoyed your recent letter immensely. Spontaneous combustion is key.
Pete

October 20, 1968 (letter from PB to LH)
Larry,

I received your first letter and wrote back some time ago. Sent it to the first address that came into mind so I don't know if you received it. Did you? As to coming home for Thanksgiving vacation—pretty much out of the question this year, sorry to say, as it comes so late. It falls between the time classes are over and exams begin. I will be back home on December 3rd in any case. Lucy is arriving (from France) at JFK on December 22nd and will come down to Washington (I will probably try to meet her in NY) and stay until the 24th when she will fly to Seattle.

Roy is planning to spend next term in Washington. Hopefully you and he can hitch out here sometime next term. I took the GRE exam, committing an entire afternoon. Felt glad at the first news of the Bomb Halt.
What's the story on the Free University???
Pete

I was looking forward to reuniting with Lucy at winter break. She had been abroad since June. After landing in New York, she took the train to D.C. to see me before heading home to Seattle for Christmas. So much had happened while she was away. Fortunately, Norman Mailer captured all the bloody good parts in *Armies of the Night* which had just come out. I gave her a copy and told her, "Here's what you missed." She was not that thrilled with the gift, anticipating, I suspect, something more personal and intimate. But it was Norman Mailer, after all.

November 1, 1968 (Letter from LH to PB)
Pete,

There is a surfeit of shit to relate. First off is the big news of the week. Jay Levy returned to the East recently—climbing through our living room window and scaring the shit out of Cooper. That night there was a big scene at our house. Dr. Hill and a lot of freaks from the PAC were there. I was out until all hours with some chick. I returned home in the a.m. and see eight million empty beer cans and a dozen overflowing ashtrays, and an abandoned pair of cowboy boots. When I awoke, there was Levy, upright, in his boots and grinning.

The funny thing was that two weeks before I had a premonition of Levy's imminent arrival. We talked or rather I made him talk of the west and his adventures and plans and etc. He had been living with a gorgeous young nurse in San Francisco. He consulted with the I Ching. That august authority told him to hop on a jet and come back. Which he did, leaving no note or forwarding address for the nurse. He is really mad of course, but somehow content with his own madness and perhaps destined to be a little happy for the rest of his life. He has that amazing long, wind-wild hair and the embryo of a beard. Perhaps he will become a mystic once his whiskers grow in. He spent that whole day with us and then took all of our best records and bussed to Silver Spring. Since then only silence. He did mention music a lot and wanted to get back into some sort of a thing with Howell and Bob B. and those freaks.

About the Free University, let me be brief. Buckeye and I decided to do it and went to the SGA for funds and support. They tried to assume the leadership and we said shove it. They gave us about thirty bucks and the use of their mimeo machine. We set up eleven courses taught by volunteer Profs. Courses such as "Drugs,", "Group Dynamics," "Dylan Thomas" and "Modern Theater," plus some sociology and psychology courses, one history course and an astronomy course.

We printed our own registration forms and the newspaper printed a special edition containing our goals and objectives as well as the Free U catalogue and course descriptions. We registered 500 people which broke all records and precedents and turned the school momentarily upside down. Lots of drops-outs by now but about six really good courses going strong.
Ca Marche,
Larry

Nixon beat Humphrey by a million votes out of 60 million cast. The unspeakable George Wallace garnered nine million. But Nixon tallied 301 electoral votes compared to Humphries' 191. It was a repudiation of everything we had worked for over the last four years. This Peace Movement was on the rocks. The country was more polarized than we had imagined. It was a dark night for us all.

I had told my parents that I couldn't support Humphrey since he was so aligned with LBJ's war. As lifelong Democrats, they hated hearing that but tended to take my provocations in stride. But I voted for him in the end, not wanting to squander my first vote.

The first (and last) edition of our underground newspaper, *Effluvia*, was published just three weeks after the election. The Earlham Post was being pressured by the administration to stick to campus issues which seemed utterly irresponsible in view of all the havoc around us. I was the editor and had plenty of help from other students, including Roy, who wrote stories, added art, edited and proofread and laid it out. The headlines read:

> *FRANZ REFUSES INDUCTION!*
> *LAW'N ORDER IN CHICAGO*
> *SUPPORT OUR BOYS—OR WON'T YOU*
> *COME HOME BEETLE BAILEY*
> *HEALTHY HINTS FROM THE HEDONIST.*

January 16, 1969 (letter from PB to LH)

Dear Larry,

Last week, I was on the plane heading west and reading The Favorite Game. Kathy was sitting by the window sleeping. I was in the aisle seat. It's hard to concentrate for very long when you are on the aisle. Stewardesses kept whipping by, brushing your shoulder ever so lightly. I think their skirts are getting shorter. Either that or their smooth but-muscular, bare and comely legs are getting longer.

Distractions aside, I wanted to say that I liked The Favorite Game which I actually dug more than the Farina book: Been Down So Long It Looks Like Up to Me, by which I kind of was insulted by because I kept thinking that he expected me to believe all that crap. Cohen did not. The only trouble with The Favorite Game was it seemed like there was no distance between the author and the narrator because it's so obviously personal. I read *Beautiful Losers* immediately afterward. It really is a terrific book. I also read *The Magus* as you suggested.

I'm taking just two courses this term—Literary Criticism is an enjoyable discussion group with only three other students and the professor, but we get hung up a lot talking about things like morality and sincerity which I'd rather avoid. Philosophy of Religion taught by a visiting true-to-life collar Jesuit priest from Fordham with a Brooklyn accent, and sounds like a really precocious cabbie. He will probably end up converting us all.

The irony is that so often New Left-types express religious concepts but can't bear to call themselves religious. A draft lawyer who was here recently said if you are a C.O. and committed to the concept of pacifism you are by definition religious (even if you profess atheism) because you are in fact appealing to a permanent, higher-order ideal. I don't know if this is true, but the course is opening up on a lot of new thoughts and ideas which are absurd not to explore.

I seem to be spending a lot of time thinking about what to do. If the draft calls remain low, I am hoping to get into a masters in teaching program at Johns Hopkins. If I start in September, I will probably stay here and work another summer for Upward Bound. If the draft gets tighter, I might try to get into the Teacher Corps

Jesus it feels weird to be thinking about the future, and the things I am thinking about have actual names and dates and such. It's becoming all too close and too real.

Pete

January 24, 1969 (letter from LH to PB)

Pete,

I just got back from an amazing weekend in Washington working with National Mobilization. National MOBE asked people from the Peace Action Comm. to get together a team to act as marshals and street organizers. I was asked if I wanted to work with Rennie Davis, and of course I said yes.

After several meetings in Baltimore, a group of us decided to spend the weekend at Mary Moyland's commune in D.C. (a huge house on F Street filled with transients, hipsters alcoholics, radicals, screaming babies, madmen, Catholic nuns etc. Very Catholic Worker-like, if you can dig it).

Cooper and I drove to the Hawthorne School for the all-day training. Assembled were all the usual groups: high school kids, acid freaks, dedicated radicals, Trotskyites, AFSC people, Biafra people, peace people and some actual Yippies, not to mention FBI agents, draft resisters and all the general human debris that is somehow attracted to the Left.

It was a wild, colorful, happy, mad scene and underneath it all, amazingly enough, the really professional organization of MOBE. After the training for the street organizers, I went to a workshop on communes and co-ops held by the Radical Action Cooperative. The next day, there was a rally followed by a 6,000-person march down Pennsylvania Avenue, That night there was a music and light festival in the tent replete with confusion, grass, huge pressing crowds of people and scenes beyond compare. There was organized chanting and heckling while Nixon and other dignitaries sped by. Later rampaging groups of super-radical (SDS, YAWF) types broke windows and tried to force confrontations.

During the weekend, of course, I met this really fine girl ("Uh oh, I'm in love again," sings Fats Domino) who also blew my skull. I can't believe how perfectly she stands up to my interior Ideal Chick scheme. More on her later.

If you go to Hopkins, why don't you plan to live in our commune? It will be in the city and should be interesting. It would also save me the trouble of hammering out all these fucking letters.

Love to Lucy Dougall, Kathy Berliner et al.

Larry

January 29, 1969 (letter from PB to LH)

Larry,

I'm fairly bursting with things to discuss, decisions to be made, lives to be formed, money to be squandered, potential to be actualized and history to be written. I'm applying to teaching programs at Oberlin, Johns Hopkins and the University of Pennsylvania. Do you like teaching now? Is it making sense to you (even in a white, suburban, system-dominated school)? What are your plans for the future? What's for dinner? What are your opinions about the stock market?

Life goes on. There is too much rain and snow. It's created gray and dreary walls inside and out. Sometimes the sun breaks through, lifts the

horizon and makes winter worthwhile. Lucy is around almost always. What an improvement, especially with Brad looking so grim these days. It's getting harder to imagine life without her. Strange and lovely.
Write.
Pete

The Draft was closing in. I didn't know how great a case I could make for being a conscientious objector. I wasn't a member of a church. I couldn't quote from the Scriptures or point to a life of sacrifice or self-flagellation. I didn't really think much about God except in the context of philosophical discussions or to invoke His name in vain. I could argue with equal assurance for both God's existence and absence.

I *appreciated* religion. I liked to visit the pomp and ritual, the holidays and festivals, and listen to gospel music, hymns, and Gregorian chants. I liked the Quakers because they eschewed all of the above. I also knew that a lot of terrible things are done by true believers. I was conflicted. I couldn't see conning my way out of the Army. Whatever path I chose had to come from a place that was real—a place of belief. Did I believe in God? It depended on one's definition. If God was a mystery, a miracle or an unspeakable truth, then God indeed existed in a perfect Miles Davis solo, in the breathtaking harmonies of The Temptations, in the sparkling prose of F. Scott Fitzgerald, and in all the places and people and creatures so beautiful that they took your breath away. Yes. There were things in the world greater and more powerful and mysterious than logic could account for. But was that enough to be called Divine? Was there unknown (and unknowable) force within the world—and within me—that required not only my attention but also my faith?

According to some, religion (or to be religious) requires the recognition of a Higher Power that determines our fate and for that reason, deserves our reverence and obedience. Others describe religion as a longing for something greater than oneself that offered a way forward—a path toward righteousness, enlightenment or nirvana, and for that reason required both our faith and devotion. I could certainly dig that.

The only thing that was clear was that I needed to find my own way. That meant believing, at a basic level, that somehow things *mattered*, and that whatever I did or aspired to do would make a difference. That I had to believe, if only because the alternative to belief was nihilism and despair.

While I was home during the semester break, Larry confided that he was in love.

> *I was at the Student Union Building sitting behind the tables we set up whenever the army recruiters came to campus, talking to students, passing out leaflets. At the same time, I'm selling grass out of those big square tins they make for Twinings English Breakfast Tea. I'd spoon out an ounce or two into baggies and close them up with twist ties, and sell that shit all day. Right at the front entrance to the Student Union.*
>
> *In the midst of it all, a beautiful brunette comes by. With her style and clothes, and the way she moved and carried herself, she really stood out from the horde of suburban girls at Towson. She was mysterious, beautiful and totally unapproachable. Of course, I fell in love immediately.*

But hadn't I heard that before?

Back at Earlham one morning, after stumbling home late Saturday night from an off-campus party the night before, Lucy, over our third cup of coffee, asked: "If you had a choice, where would you go? The beach or the mountains?" I could tell that there was something important in the way she said it. I thought a bit. Having grown up in Maryland, I always liked going to Ocean City or Rehoboth or the Chesapeake Bay. Playing in the waves. Laying out on the warm sand. Walking the boardwalks. And almost always returning with a first-degree sunburn that left me writhing in pain. I also liked being in the woods, but I didn't know much about the mountains outside of hiking a few lazy trails in the Alleghenies.

"The mountains," I said.

This, apparently, was the correct answer. Lucy was from Seattle. Though she spent a lot of summers on the New Jersey shore, she was more northwest than east coast. Her family was an adventurous crew. Her father was a high school physics teacher and mountain climber. He used the summers and an occasional sabbatical to travel the world. Lucy had spent a year in Australia when she was young, and another in Chile as a teen while her father taught in a local school. They hiked and camped and skied wherever they went, ventured on wilderness treks and spent many a night freezing in tents. It was all quite fascinating.

"That's great," she said. "So would I."

I guess it was then that I began to envision in earnest a different future for myself, leaving the familiar behind, and exploring new worlds with Lucy.

May 6, 1969 (letter from PB to LH)

Larry,

The news of your marriage (marriage!) to Rosemary invokes the Great Muse. Were I a potter, I would throw a pot or a bowl or a teacup or two. Or any kind of craftsman, I would build a cabinet or make a barrel (were I a barrel maker) as a humble tribute to love.

What are the plans? I expect to be home on the 9th of June. Kathy and Lucy are up in the air about coming. I think they want to know if you want them to come. I'm sure you do. Will Levy be there? Will Gloria and Buddy? Will Miss Ruddle???

Write when you first get five minutes free.

Pete

May 18, 1969 (letter from LH to PB)

Pete

First of all, let me apologize for not writing, but I have been busy with incredibly nonsensical preparations for my impending nuptials. Busy with frantic arrangements for the commune (known to lawyers, bankers and the unhip public as the Institute for Social Research of which I am the official president). Tired because teaching is tiring. Waking up at 6:30 a.m. is really what is tiring. Teaching can be fine in certain ways. Talking with kids about books is fine, but talking to other teachers (high school English) is depressing.

But nice things do happen. Nice in the way J.D. Salinger used that word, referring to simple, and meaningful but everyday sort of things that make the absurd tolerable. Your two letters were nice, very nice as a matter fact. The first brought joy, tears held back and warmth. It was full of love and very important and memorable for me (and for us). The second letter was somewhat embarrassing in a difficult to explain way, but thank you, thank you, thank you for both letters. They were nice.

Last weekend was insane and indicative of why I'm less than impressed with Philip Roth than most people. I took Rosemary home on Saturday afternoon, and in about 24 hours she met and was examined by no less than (by actual count) thirty Jewish people—mostly relatives. The list included Buzzy and his wife Lucy, Ellie and Hal, Aunt Dottie, Uncle Nate, Grandma Rose and Uncle Bill, my parents, my brothers, family, friends, real estate agents, my father's salesman and Sissy from New York, baby cousins, Jack's pals from high school and more.

The heroes of this piece were my brothers and my mother and my Aunt Sissy. Helen and Bill (rich, childless couple from New York <u>and</u> Miami and who are exactly like the couple in Rosemary's Baby) laid $200 on us. I had anticipated this and cut my hair. But I saved my integrity by telling the assembled guests as much while my parents hid their grimaces in extra loud guffaws. All in all, it was a crazy weekend.

On the way home, I turned to Rosemary and asked her what she thought of the whole experience. She said "Jewish people <u>do</u> talk funny," and launched into a remarkably accurate rendition of a New York nasal Jewish dialect, "So, how are ya'?"

I frequently do nothing but grin like a fool these days. I read Goodbye Columbus and Portnoy's Complaint but I am left unmoved. I have lived that shit for two decades.

Cooper, Ickes and Poulis are now classified 4-F. Apparently, it's easy to convince these military snoids that you are a drug fiend and potential freak-out. Cooper did about a nine-day speed run in preparation for the physical. When the sergeant asked him what drugs he was using, Cooper asked, "Do you want me to list them alphabetically, by frequency or by quantity?" At that point he was told to get the fuck out.

I finished my C.O. application and sent it to Local Board #53. Now we just wait. I want you to see what I wrote but I want to be there while you read it. I plan to show up about a day or two before your graduation by myself and I'll bring it with me. Please convince Kathy and Lucy of the importance of their presence at my and Rosemary's union. I want all the people I love around for this event. God knows that you all are on the top of that list.

Larry

Larry and Rosemary were married in a Catholic church in Silver Spring. He promised to love, honor and obey—and whatever else Catholics required. How he evolved from a wise-assed seventh grader to a man fit for matrimony baffled me. But I guessed if he could do it, I could too.

On the day before my graduation. Lucy and I sat on the grass outside of Carpenter Hall. Dad and Mother would arrive that evening and stay for the ceremony. I was planning to return to Silver Spring with them, pick up Dick's VW Bug and head to Oberlin to start the Masters in teaching program. Lucy had another term to complete before she graduated. I guess I could have gone off into the sunset as far as the two of us were concerned. But it was the last thing I wanted to do.

"I want you to come to Oberlin when you graduate," I told her.

"That would be great," she said. "But that's kind of a big commitment."

"I'm committed if you are."

"Really? You are not exactly known for commitment. You're better known for drifting away."

"Says who?"

"Everyone."

"That was then."

"What are you saying?"

"I'm saying that when you graduate, you should join me at Oberlin."

She stared at me and didn't say a word.

"Well. What's the answer?"

"Usually you have to ask a question before you get an answer."

There was an awkward pause. In the space between the words _will_ and _you_, I was struck by a vision of the girls I would never love, the places I might never see, the paths I would never travel. But just then I saw that _she_ was the one I loved. _She_ was who I wanted to be with. _This_ was the path I want to take. _This_ was the life I was choosing.

I posed a question that might have surprised me as much as her.

"Yes," she answered. "I will."

Later, we decided to get married that December in the same Quaker Meeting House where her parents were wed 25 years before.

Chapter 12

I couldn't procrastinate any longer. A week after graduating, I sent in my application to be classified as a conscientious objector. If it was approved, and I was drafted, I would be required to spend the next two years performing community service work for poverty wages.

I wasn't all that confident. But I was certain that war—and especially this war—was wrong, and that renouncing the use of arms was not only right, it was necessary. If my application was rejected, there was nothing that would prevent my induction—no flat feet, heart murmurs or night blindness. That left two options: fleeing to Canada or going to jail.

I spent the summer at Oberlin College, taking classes with a cohort of prospective teachers. It was an eventful summer. Apollo 11 blasted off from the Kennedy Space Center on July 16th and six days later, Neil Armstrong set foot on the moon. At almost the same time, some of the best minds of my generation were getting blown away at Woodstock— three days of music, drugs, rain, mud, bacchanalia and dysentery. I wished I was there.

I found an apartment in a house close to the campus where Lucy would come visit me in the fall and move in for good after we married.

Grad School
Classes at Oberlin were cancelled on October 15th in solidarity with antiwar demonstrations that were planned across the country. I joined other Oberlin students in a short trip to Elyria, one of the many working class towns providing human fodder for the war. On arriving, we handed out fliers inviting people to the rally at the courthouse at noon.

An elderly woman asked why I wasn't fighting for my country. I told her I was, and she hurried off. Another asked if I was trying to keep myself out of the war. "Yes," I said. She said she had a son over there now. I said we were trying to bring him back. She said she hoped we would. A girl handed me a note that said, "Keep America beautiful – get off the streets."

About a hundred people were at the rally. A minister spoke first and others followed. While they were speaking, I talked to a union member who said he had already done his time in the service, but if he was asked to go to Vietnam, he'd go to Leavenworth instead.

A young woman said, "Those Vietnamese are ignorant and live like animals, so why should I oppose the war?"

After the rally, we marched to the draft board. When we got there, we all sat down in the street hoping we'd get arrested. People sang *I Ain't Goin' to Study War No More* and *All We Are Saying is Give Peace a Chance*. One of the protestors stepped forward and put a match to his draft card. The singing stopped. There was a hush. He held the card by its corner. It took a long time to burn. The kid next to me said, "That fool has a lot of guts." There were cheers, and the singing got louder. We all held up our fingers in a V for peace.

I doubt that the demonstration changed anyone's mind. Political positions seemed fast and hardened. But I returned to Oberlin sobered and inspired by the day's events certain that ending the war might require something extreme.

The Moratorium March

It was snowing hard on the road through Pennsylvania on our way to D.C. Five of us were crammed into an old Plymouth Duster with a balky heater. I wondered if anyone had checked the tires for tread. We arrived around ten that night. I made my way to my parents' house. Lucy and Kathy were already there. We were all excited about joining what we expected to be a massive peace action.

The next morning, Dad dropped us off close to the National Mall. He spent the rest of the morning giving rides to other marchers. There were a half million demonstrators—an unsteady coalition of liberals, radicals, Yippies and pacifists collectively referred to as the *New Left*. We stood for hours in the cold listening to stirring speeches by McCarthy and McGovern, and songs by Peter, Paul and Mary, Arlo Guthrie and Pete Seeger. We had heard them before, but this time everyone seemed more somber, resolute and angry. It was peaceful nonetheless. Nixon spent the day holed up in the White House, behind a barricade of buses and a battalion of police.

The Lottery

On a Wednesday night in December, I joined the other graduate students to watch the National Draft Lottery on TV. There would be no more deferments. Everyone would be on equal footing. It was to become a crap shoot for everyone.

We passed around a jug of Mountain Chablis which we drank hastily in an effort to quell our nerves. The announcer said that *Mayberry RFD* will not be aired tonight because of this special broadcast. The camera shifted to a woman in front of a box full of plastic capsules each representing a different date. The sooner your birthday was picked, the more likely you would be drafted. It was projected that anyone whose birth date was drawn in the first third would surely be called.

The countdown was slow and tortuous. There was no room for error. The first fifty went called. Then fifty more. I was feeling good until it reached 116. Then it was over for me.

A Wedding

Lucy and I were married two days after Christmas at the Friends Meeting House in Clarksboro, N.J. It snowed furiously on the day before the wedding. A weather emergency was declared in New England. Even so, a lot of brave souls made the trip including Cooper, Larry and Rosemary, and

Larry's parents and brothers. Jay appeared without word of warning. Only Bob was missing, probably because I had lost track of his address.

It was a Quaker ceremony which was mostly silent. Quakers always provide space for people to listen to and speak from their hearts. There was no minister or judge to conduct the proceedings. Lucy and I sat facing all the people who had gathered, and who sat silently meditating or simply wondering what was going on. We endured the quiet as long as we could. Then Lucy and I rose. I made a traditional Quaker vow:

> *In the presence of God and before these our families and friends, I take thee to be my wife, promising with Divine assistance to be unto thee a loving and faithful husband so long as we both shall live.*

After Lucy said hers, we signed the marriage certificate and sat down. It was silent for a while more. Her father and others made poignant remarks. Afterward, everyone signed the marriage certificate as our witnesses.

It was all a blur. I felt like I was stepping through a passageway to adulthood, and I could hear the sound of a door slamming behind me. Over the past four years, distance, geographical and otherwise, between me and the pals of my youth, had grown. I knew that my future lay westward, even farther from the people who had helped me come of age. It was a wistful feeling.

Later there was a raucous reception in the refurbished barn at Lucy's grandparents' farm. There was a lot of champagne, and lots of music and dancing. People of all ages attempted the Limbo. Uncle Buzzy fell flat on his back. It was a great party.

The next morning, Lucy and I drove my borrowed Volkswagen through the slush onto the New Jersey Turnpike, and northward over the snow covered New England landscape to Stowe, Vermont. We stayed for several days with Lucy's friend Hansell and her family. I tried skiing for the first time and got to drive a snowmobile. We celebrated the New

Year by drinking hot toddies in front of a roaring fire, the windows opaque with frost. On New Year's Day, the first of the new decade, we drove back to Oberlin to begin our lives anew. I was about to begin teaching recalcitrant high school students about the wonders of literature. It was time to put childish things behind me.

End of the Decade

The Sixties were born in idealism and expired in despair. The struggle for racial justice was never won. In spite of the protests, the war raged on. The spirit of Woodstock had devolved into the nightmare of Altamont, where a Hell's Angel stabbed a teenager to death 20 feet from where the Rolling Stones were blasting out *Under My Thumb*. The optimism of the student movement was dealt a final blow when National Guardsmen killed two student protesters at Jackson State University, just eleven days after four students were gunned down at Kent State. But seeds of change were sown. Other movements sprang up, took hold, and grew in the years to come.

If this was a novel, I'd close it by describing how Jay was re-conscripted into the Army and perished in Vietnam in the Battle of Hue. That Cooper, after surviving a motorcycle crash high in the Andes lived as a holy man deep in a Peruvian jungle. That Bob Ochsman joined the army, became a three-star general and was later named as the director of Homeland Security. That Larry, after relentless pursuit by the FBI, was gunned down along with a dozen Grey Panthers in a battle over Social Security. And me? I became a foreign correspondent and sent dispatches home from battlefields in Grenada.

But reality is never as exciting as fantasy. In truth, we all slipped irretrievably into the Ordinary. We went on being just who we were—our lives the sum total of an infinitesimal number of decisions which, if we had been given the chance to revisit, would have undoubtedly been the same.

All in all, the ordinary is not such a bad place to be. We all married. We had kids. Some of us divorced and remarried. We experienced joys and sorrows, births and deaths, good health and bad. Through it all, our friendship survived.

Cooper did, in fact, take a solo motorcycle journey through North Africa and the Middle East. Later, he married Laurie and they had a daughter, Rachel, who lives and works in Sweden. After many years alone, Cooper met and married Walda. They now live near Washington D.C. He still rides a vintage BMW motorcycle, travels across the world for deep sea diving adventures and volunteers as a crew member on racing yachts. He plans to take up the guitar again soon.

Bob graduated from the University of North Carolina and earned his PhD at Johns Hopkins University. He married Bobbie, and settled in Little Rock where he was a psychology professor and department chair at the University of Arkansas, before going to work for IBM and later the federal government. They had two children. Today, they live on a small horse farm with a spectacular view of the Blue Ridge Mountains. Bob is spending his retirement restoring classic sports cars, among other pursuits.

Jay lived in San Francisco and pursued a music career with some success. He recorded an album with the band called *Melton, Levy and the Dey Brothers* that was produced by Michael Bloomfield. He later returned to Washington with his wife, Valerie, and eventually took over his father's pawn shop. Jay and Valerie had four children. Today, he struggles with Parkinson's disease. He still attends our periodic reunions, and tells the best stories of our time together in the 60s.

Like me, Larry became a conscientious objector during Vietnam. Again, like me, he married while still in college and had two kids fairly quickly. He later earned a Master's degree in Social Work and ran programs for troubled kids and teens for many years. He divorced and then married Becky and they adopted two girls. In the early 90s, he made a career change and became a marketing writer for several healthcare companies. At one point he bought and operated a coffee-shop in Baltimore called *The Daily Grind*.

After I finished the teaching program at Oberlin College, Lucy and I moved to Boulder where I fulfilled my obligations as a Conscientious Objector (yes, my application was approved) by working in a youth shelter. This led to a lifelong career working with social service, advocacy and philanthropic organizations. After the birth of our daughter, Jessica, we moved to Seattle to put down roots and attend graduate school. Our son, Nick, was born in 1975. After 15 years together, Lucy and I decided to divorce. In 1987, I married Melinda and we expanded our family to include our son, Nate. Our family now also includes our two grandchildren, and a wealth of siblings, cousins and kin from our combined families.

Epilogue

Bob and I leapt down the stairs (as much as a couple of old guys can leap) to see if Jay survived the fall. At least he was breathing. Then he began to moan.

"Are you all right?" I asked.

Still wincing, he opened his eyes. "It hurts," he said.

"I'm sorry, Jay," I said. I was sorry for not stopping him from falling or being there to soften the blow, not only then but through the years.

"Just give me a minute," he said. Bob got some ice and held it tenderly against his head. He continued to moan. At last, he said, "That was one small step for a man. And one giant kick in the ass for me."

Cooper called down from the top of the stairs. "Is Levy OK?"

"Compared to what?" I yelled back. "It wasn't like he was in great shape when he got here."

I knew that he hurt all over but somehow he braved the pain. "Help me up," he said.

We helped him stand, then we carefully brought him up the stairs and eased him into a chair.

Cooper got out beer and potato chips. There was stillness. Then Larry broke the ice, unleashing a flood of chatter and stories that lasted into the night. We laughed until our sides ached. We talked until the words no longer flowed.

The comfort we felt being together was palpable. There was much to say, but words could not convey all that we were thinking or feeling.

After college, Larry, Jay, Cooper and I were periodically in touch. Each of them came to visit me in Seattle at least once. Family and work obligations frequently brought me back East where I would see one or all of them. Over the years, we celebrated the births of our children and commiserated over whatever calamities life threw at us.

I had not seen Bob for thirty years, but he and Jay had reconnected. This was the first time since the 60s that all five of us were in one place.

The talk that day was about old times and new. Cooper told a funny and frightening story about parasailing into the side of a barn. Bob explained how he came to own a collection of matching red sports cars that included a Ferrari, a Mustang, two Corvettes and a dune buggy. Jay recounted a number of crazy, gut-busting tales about Sam's Pawn Shop—enough to warrant a whole other book.

The conversation might have turned to a recital of complaints about the indignities of aging. But we refrained. We didn't need to be reminded that we were light years from our youth.

We all were older, but in Jay we saw the future. It wasn't a pretty sight. I could live with becoming slower and creakier. But I was not prepared for the possibility of becoming infirm.

Seeing him was all the more poignant because he had always been the most vibrant and gifted among us. He reminded me still of the line from *Richard Cory*,

> *In fine, we thought that he was everything*
> *To make us wish that we were in his place.*

In the waning hours, as the empty bottles accumulated, we relived the best parts of our youth. How was it possible to feel this close after so many years? But it should not have been a surprise. These men who once were boys were ineffably special to me and to each other. Our friendships were entwined with all that I ever knew of innocence, yearning and joy.

Ever so slowly, the sky darkened. The stars came out. One more story? Another drink? A last cigarette?

It was time to take Jay home—albeit somewhat worse for wear. As always, I didn't know when I would see him again or what the future would bring. But I knew that being there for him and for each other was as important to me as it ever was.

We exchanged farewells. "Love you guys," we said quickly the way men do. "Let's do this again."

Then we went our separate ways.

Acknowledgements

Many thanks to my friends and siblings who populate this memoir and permitted me to share whatever I chose about them. Thank you also to Larry, Jay and my brother Dick for writing such compelling and heartfelt letters and permitting me to reprint them, and to Larry for preserving the letters I sent him so many years ago. Letters, like wine and baseball cards, grow more precious with age. They create a permanent record in the way that e-mails, texts and tweets can never do (unless, of course, you are under indictment). Everyone! Please write!

I want to acknowledge the contributions of all those who were willing to wade through my drafts and provide suggestions: Barbara Erwine, Sorrel North, Michelle Domash, Bob Meinig, Barbara Padden, John Cell, Jessica Berliner, Cliff Freed and Mary Meinig. It was a group effort, and I appreciate all (or most) of your suggestions and corrections. Thank you Barbara for designing the cover.

I am especially appreciative of and grateful to Melinda, my partner in all things, who encouraged, inspired, and put up with me throughout the long process of creating and then recreating this book. Thank you. I'm indebted to you, as always.

Finally, much thanks to Hugo House in Seattle for its support for both new and seasoned writers.

Peter Berliner

December 2017

Made in the USA
Middletown, DE
21 November 2018